WORD MASTERY 2026

FROM BEGINNER TO EXPERT

THE ULTIMATE GUIDE TO FEATURES, FUNCTIONS, AND PRODUCTIVITY TIPS

TABLE OF CONTENTS

INTRODUCTION

Welcome to the ultimate guide to Microsoft Word, a powerful tool designed to revolutionize how you create, edit, and collaborate on documents. Whether you're drafting a professional report, a school essay, or a personal project, this guide will equip you with the skills to unlock Word's full potential.

I.   WHY WORD MATTERS

Microsoft Word has been at the forefront of digital document creation for decades, offering a reliable and versatile platform. As part of the Microsoft 365 suite, Word combines traditional strengths with modern innovations, enabling seamless collaboration, enhanced productivity, and accessibility from virtually any device. In today's fast-paced world, mastering Word is an essential skill for personal, professional, and academic success.

II.   WHAT IT CAN DO

Microsoft Word is more than a word processor; it's a comprehensive tool for document creation and management. With Word, you can:

- Design polished documents with professional-quality templates and formatting tools.
- Collaborate in real-time with colleagues and peers using cloud integration.
- Automate repetitive tasks with advanced features like macros and Mail Merge.
- Ensure inclusivity with cutting-edge accessibility tools and features.
- Share, secure, and manage files across devices.

This guide is structured to help you:

- **Navigate the Word Environment**: Learn the layout, tools, and features that make Word user-friendly and efficient.

- **Create and Format Documents**: Explore tools for crafting visually appealing and well-structured content.

- **Collaborate and Share**: Master real-time co-authoring, commenting, and sharing options.

- **Harness Advanced Features**: Use Mail Merge, macros, and automation to save time and boost productivity.

- **Solve Common Challenges**: Troubleshoot issues and leverage Word's powerful features to streamline your workflow.

CHAPTER 1: GETTING STARTED WITH WORD

I. INSTALLING AND LAUNCHING WORD

Installing and launching Microsoft Word as part of Microsoft 365 is straightforward. This section will guide you through the process to ensure you have Word set up and ready to use on your device.

1. INSTALLING MICROSOFT WORD

i. Microsoft 365 Subscription:

1. Visit the Microsoft 365 website (www.microsoft.com/en/ microsoft-365) to purchase a subscription or sign in if you already have one.
2. Choose the plan that best suits your needs (e.g., Personal, Family, or Business).

ii. Download and Installation:

1. After purchasing a subscription, sign in with your Microsoft account.
2. Go to the **Services & Subscriptions** section, and select **Install Office**.
3. Download the Office installer and run it on your device.
4. Follow the on-screen instructions to complete the installation process.

iii. Mobile Devices:

1. Download the Microsoft Word app from the Google Play Store (Android) or the Apple App Store (iOS).

2. Sign in with your Microsoft 365 account to activate premium features.

2. Launching Microsoft Word

i. On Desktop:

1. Open the **Start Menu** (Windows) or **Applications Folder** (Mac).
2. Search for "Microsoft Word" and click to launch.
3. Alternatively, pin Word to your Taskbar or Dock for quick access.

ii. On Mobile:

1. Tap the Word app icon on your smartphone or tablet.
2. Sign in with your Microsoft 365 credentials to access your documents.

iii. Cloud Integration:

1. When launching Word, connect it to OneDrive for seamless access to your cloud-saved files.
2. Use the **Recent Documents** list to quickly open previously edited files.

II. THE WORD ENVIRONMENT: RIBBON, TOOLBAR, AND NAVIGATION PANE

Microsoft Word introduces a modernized and user-friendly interface designed to streamline your document creation process. This section will guide you through the essential components of the Word environment to ensure you are comfortable navigating and using its features effectively.

1. THE RIBBON

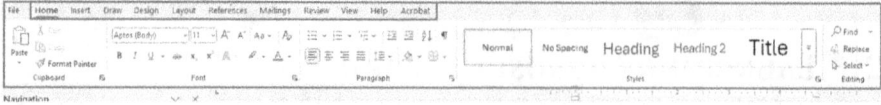

Figure 1.   **Word Ribbon.png**

The Ribbon is the central hub for all commands and tools in Word. It is organized into tabs, each focusing on a specific aspect of document creation and editing. Key tabs include:

- **Home**: Basic text formatting, paragraph alignment, and clipboard functions.
- **Insert**: Tools for adding tables, pictures, shapes, charts, and more.
- **Layout**: Adjust page setup, margins, and spacing.
- **References**: Add citations, tables of contents, and footnotes.
- **Review**: Check spelling, track changes, and collaborate with others.

2. QUICK ACCESS TOOLBAR

The toolbar houses frequently used tools and can be customized for your workflow. By default, the Quick Access Toolbar includes shortcuts like Save, Undo, and Redo. You can add or remove commands to match your preferences.

Figure 2.   **Word Toolbar.png**

3. THE NAVIGATION PANE

This powerful feature simplifies navigating large documents.

- **View the Navigation Pane**: Go to the **View** tab and check the **Navigation Pane** box.
- **Browse by Headings**: Jump between sections easily using your document's headings.
- **Search**: Quickly find specific text or phrases in your

document.

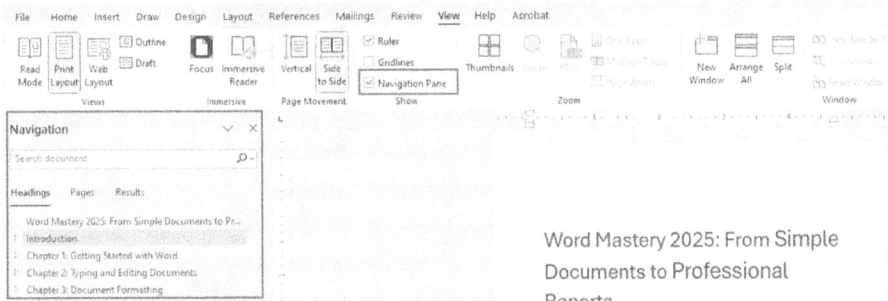

Figure 3. **Word Navigation Pane.png**

4. STATUS BAR

Located at the bottom of the Word window, the status bar provides quick insights about your document, including:

- Page and word count.
- View options (e.g., Print Layout, Web Layout). You can right-click the status bar to customize what information is displayed.

Page and Word count   View Options   Zoom slider

Figure 4. **Status bar.png**

5. CUSTOMIZING THE WORD ENVIRONMENT

Tailor Word to suit your needs: you can personalize your theme Word environment to show commands and tabs you use frequently and hide the ones you use less often.

Under the **File** menu, select **Options > General.** From there, you can customize Theme, Ribbon, Language, Display settings, Quick Access Toolbar, etc.

III. WORKING ON THE WORD START SCREEN

1. NAVIGATING THE WORD START SCREEN

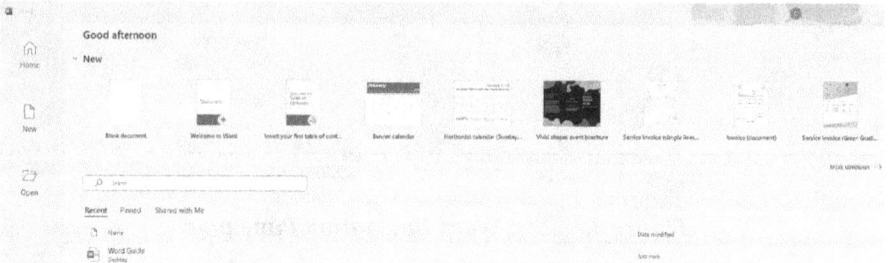

Figure 6.   ***Word Start Screen.jpg***

The Start Screen appears when you open Word, providing several options to begin your work.

- **Recent Documents**: Quickly access files you've worked on recently.
- **Templates**: Choose a pre-designed template for common document types like resumes or reports.
- **New Blank Document**: Click on the **Blank Document** icon to start fresh.
- **Search for Templates**: Use the search bar to find templates that match your needs (e.g., "Invoice" or "Newsletter").

2. CREATING YOUR FIRST DOCUMENT

Starting from Scratch:

1. Select **Blank Document** from the Start Screen.
2. Begin typing in the main workspace, also known as the canvas.

Using a Template:

1. Select a template that fits your needs.

2. Customize the text, formatting, and design elements as needed.

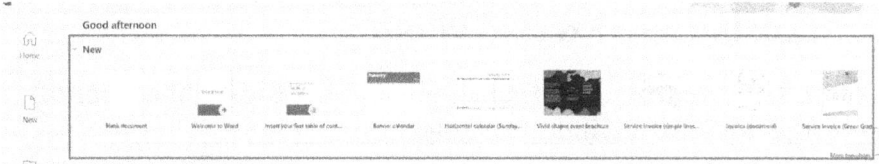

Figure 7.   Create a new document.png

Open a document:

1. Double-click on the document to open it.

2. Press Ctrl + O to open the options. From here, you can quickly open the recent documents or browse the locations of the documents you need.

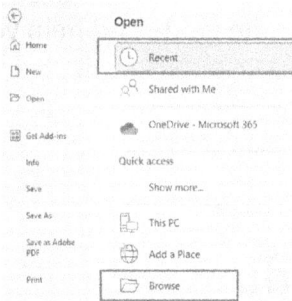

Figure 8.   Open a Word file.png

3. SAVING YOUR WORK

Saving for the First Time:

1. Go to **File > Save As** or click **Save** or press **Ctrl + S** (Windows) or **Command+S** (Mac).

2. Choose a location (e.g., your computer or OneDrive) and name your file.

3. Select a file format (default: **DOCX**).

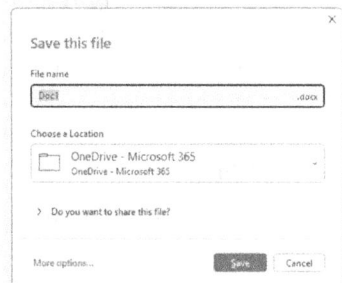

AutoSave: Ensure AutoSave is enabled for files saved on OneDrive or SharePoint to avoid losing progress.

4. CLOSING AND EXITING WORD

- **Close the Document**: Click the **X** in the top-right corner of the document window or select **File > Close**.
- **Exit Word**: Close all open documents and click the **X** in the application window.

IV. WORD TERMINOLOGY: PARAGRAPHS, STYLES, SECTIONS, AND HEADERS

Before diving deeper into using Microsoft Word, it's essential to understand some of its core terminology. These terms will frequently appear throughout the guide and help you navigate Word with ease.

1. PARAGRAPHS

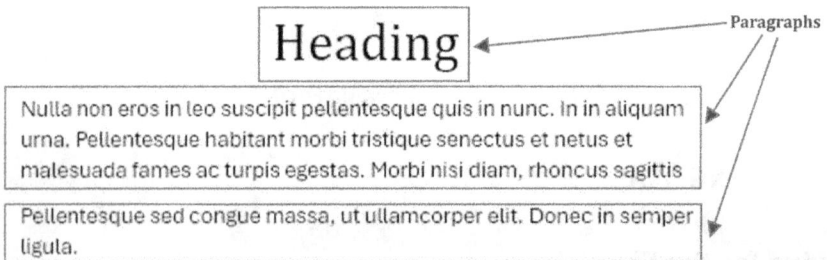

Heading ← Paragraphs

Nulla non eros in leo suscipit pellentesque quis in nunc. In in aliquam urna. Pellentesque habitant morbi tristique senectus et netus et malesuada fames ac turpis egestas. Morbi nisi diam, rhoncus sagittis

Pellentesque sed congue massa, ut ullamcorper elit. Donec in semper ligula.

In Word, a paragraph is defined as any text followed by a hard return (pressing the Enter key). Paragraphs are the building blocks of documents and can be formatted individually.

- **Formatting Options**: Line spacing, indentation, and alignment.
- **Uses**: Create headings, body text, bullet points, or numbered lists.

2. STYLES

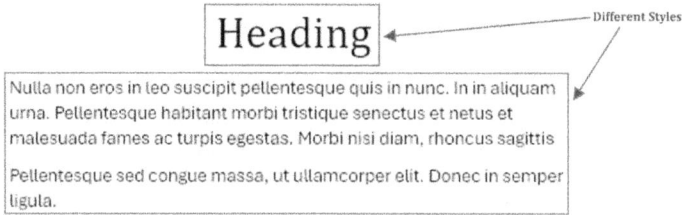

Figure 9.   *Styles.png*

Styles are pre-defined sets of formatting options you can apply to text, paragraphs, or tables.

- **Types**: Heading styles, normal styles, and custom styles.
- **Benefits**: Ensures consistency throughout the document and speeds up formatting.
- **How to Apply**: Go to the **Home** tab and select from the **Styles Gallery**.

3. HEADERS AND FOOTERS

Headers appear at the top of each page, and footers appear at the bottom. They are used for consistent elements like page numbers, document titles, or dates.

Figure 10.   *Header and Footer.png*

4. SECTIONS

Sections divide your document into parts, allowing for different formatting settings (e.g., margins, headers, or footers) in each section.

5. FILE FORMATS

Microsoft Word supports a variety of file formats for saving and sharing documents. Common formats include:

- **DOCX**: The default format for Word documents.
- **PDF**: Ideal for sharing documents while preserving formatting.
- **RTF**: A basic text format compatible with most text editors.
- **Plain Text (TXT)**: A format without any formatting, ideal for plain text storage.

V. SETTING WORD ASIDE: USING WORD ON CLOUD PLATFORMS

Microsoft Word isn't just for desktops; it's designed to work seamlessly across devices with Cloud integration. This flexibility allows you to create, edit, and collaborate on documents anytime, anywhere.

1. USING WORD WITH CLOUD INTEGRATION

i. OneDrive Integration:

- Save your documents to **OneDrive** to ensure they are accessible across devices.
- Real-time syncing means changes are updated instantly, whether on desktop, mobile, or the web.

ii. Accessing Word Online:

- Open a browser and go to Office.com.
- Log in with your Microsoft 365 credentials.

- Use the web version of Word to edit documents directly without downloading the software.

iii. Benefits of Cloud-Based Word:

- **Real-Time Collaboration**: Work with teammates on the same document simultaneously.
- **Autosave**: Never lose progress as Word automatically saves your changes to the cloud.
- **Version History**: Access and restore previous versions of your document as needed.

2. SWITCHING BETWEEN PLATFORMS

Word ensures a smooth transition across devices. You can start drafting a document on your desktop, then continue editing on your smartphone during your commute, and present or finalize the document using a tablet or web browser.

3. MAXIMIZING MOBILITY AND FLEXIBILITY

To make the most of Word's mobile and cloud capabilities:

- Keep your devices synced with the same Microsoft 365 account.
- Use the **Share** button to send links or collaborate on cloud-stored documents.

Figure 11.   Share button.png

CHAPTER 2: TYPING & EDITING DOCUMENTS

Mastering the basics of typing and formatting in Microsoft Word is fundamental to creating professional and visually appealing documents. This section will guide you through the essentials, helping you type efficiently and apply basic formatting to enhance your content.

I.   BASIC WORD TYPING

1.   TYPING TEXT

Start Typing:

- Click anywhere on the document canvas and begin typing.
- Press **Enter** to start a new paragraph and **Tab** to indent text.

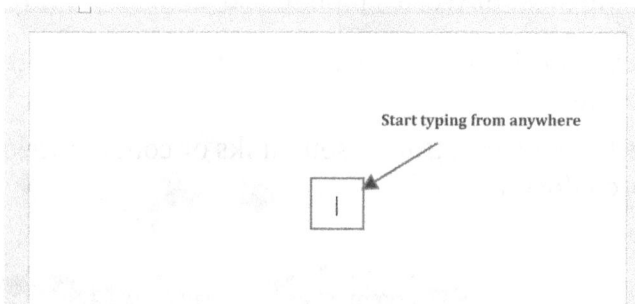

Start typing from anywhere

Figure 12.   Start Typing.png

Navigating Text:

- Use the arrow keys to move the cursor within your text.
- Hold **Ctrl** (Windows) or **Command** (Mac) while using the arrow keys to jump between words or lines.

2. FORMATTING TEXT: FONTS, COLORS, AND SIZES

Basic formatting options are available in the **Home** tab under the **Font** group.

Font Style and Size:

1. Select your text and choose a font and size from the dropdown menus.
2. Use the **Increase Font Size** or **Decrease Font Size** buttons for quick adjustments.

Bold, Italic, Underline:

1. Highlight the text and click **B** (Bold), **I** (Italic), or **U** (Underline) in the toolbar.
2. Keyboard Shortcuts:
   » **Bold**: **Ctrl+B** (Windows) or **Command+B** (Mac).
   » **Italic**: **Ctrl+I** (Windows) or **Command+I** (Mac).
   » **Underline**: **Ctrl+U** (Windows) or **Command+U** (Mac).

Text Color: select your text, click the **Font Color** icon (a colored "A"), and choose a color from the palette.

Highlighting: use the **Text Highlight Color** tool to draw attention to specific words or sentences.

Figure 13.   ***Basic text formatting.png***

3. PARAGRAPH ALIGNMENT, INDENTATION, AND SPACING

Properly aligning and spacing paragraphs ensures your document is easy to read and visually appealing.

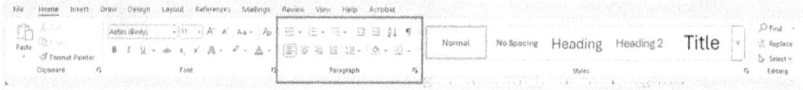

Figure 14. **Basic paragraph formatting.png**

Paragraph Alignment

You can align text in different ways to suit the purpose of your content:

- **Left Alignment** (default): Aligns text to the left margin. Shortcut: **Ctrl+L** (Windows) or **Command+L** (Mac).

- **Center Alignment**: Aligns text to the center of the page. Shortcut: **Ctrl+E** (Windows) or **Command+E** (Mac).

- **Right Alignment**: Aligns text to the right margin. Shortcut: **Ctrl+R** (Windows) or **Command+R** (Mac).

- **Justify**: Aligns text evenly across the left and right margins for a polished look. Shortcut: **Ctrl+J** (Windows) or **Command+J** (Mac).

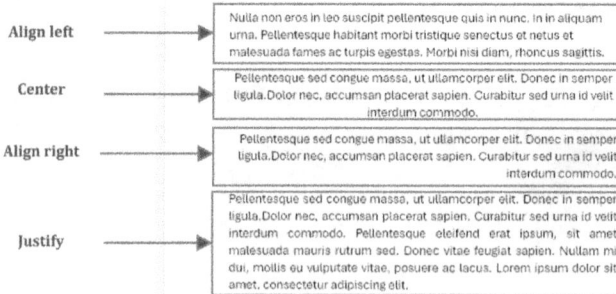

Figure 15. **Text Alignment.png**

Indentation

Control how far text is indented from the margins:

- **None:** Indents the entire paragraph.
- **First Line Indent**: Indents only the first line of a paragraph.

Use the ruler or go to **Home > Paragraph > Indentation**.

- **Hanging Indent**: Indents all lines except the first line of a paragraph. Commonly used for bibliographies and citations.

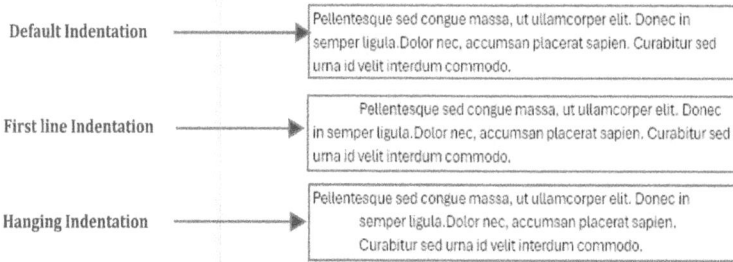

Default Indentation	Pellentesque sed congue massa, ut ullamcorper elit. Donec in semper ligula.Dolor nec, accumsan placerat sapien. Curabitur sed urna id velit interdum commodo.
First line Indentation	Pellentesque sed congue massa, ut ullamcorper elit. Donec in semper ligula.Dolor nec, accumsan placerat sapien. Curabitur sed urna id velit interdum commodo.
Hanging Indentation	Pellentesque sed congue massa, ut ullamcorper elit. Donec in semper ligula.Dolor nec, accumsan placerat sapien. Curabitur sed urna id velit interdum commodo.

Figure 16.   Indentation.png

Line Spacing

Adjust the amount of space between lines for better readability:

1. Go to **Home > Paragraph > Line and Paragraph Spacing**.
2. Choose options like **1.0 (Single), 1.5,** or **2.0 (Double)**.
3. For custom spacing, select **Line Spacing Options**.

4. BULLETED AND NUMBERED LISTS

Organizing information into lists makes your document easier to read and understand.

Bulleted Lists

Use bullet points to create an unordered list:

1. Go to the **Home** tab and click the **Bullets** icon.

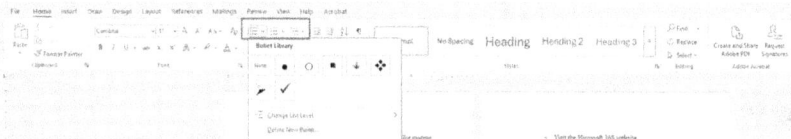

2. Type your items, pressing **Enter** after each one.
3. Customize bullets by clicking the dropdown menu next to the **Bullets** icon.

Numbered Lists

Use numbers for ordered lists, such as steps or priorities:

1. Click the **Numbering** icon in the **Home** tab.
2. Start typing your list, pressing **Enter** after each item.
3. Customize numbering styles (e.g., Roman numerals or letters) using the dropdown menu.

Nested Lists

Create sub-levels within a list:

1. Press **Tab** to indent and create a sub-item under a list.
2. Use **Shift+Tab** to move the item back to the main level.

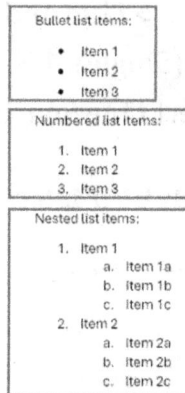

Figure 17.   **List items.png**

5. SAVING TIME WITH FORMAT PAINTER

The **Format Painter** is a powerful tool for quickly applying consistent formatting to your text.

How to Use Format Painter

1. Select the text with the formatting you want to copy.
2. Click the Format Painter icon in the Home tab (a paintbrush icon). For multiple uses, double-click the icon to lock it.

3. Highlight the text or object you want to apply the formatting to.

Figure 18.   Format Painter.png

When to Use Format Painter

- Copy formatting for headings, titles, or specific text styles.
- Apply consistent styles to bullet points, numbered lists, or table elements.
- Save time when working on large documents with repeated formatting needs.

6. INSERTING PAGE BREAKS MANUALLY AND REMOVING PAGE BREAKS

Page breaks allow you to start a new page without filling the current one, giving you control over your document's layout.

Inserting Page Breaks Manually

1. Place your cursor where you want to start a new page.
2. Go to the **Insert** tab and select **Page Break**, or use the shortcut **Ctrl+Enter** (Windows) or **Command+Enter** (Mac).

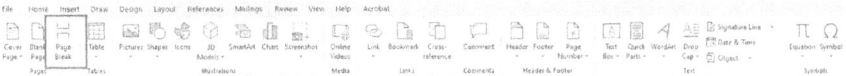

Figure 19.   Page Break.png

3. Word will immediately start a new page from the cursor's position.

Why Use Page Breaks?

- To start a new chapter or section on a fresh page.
- To separate content like tables or images from text.

Removing Page Breaks

1. Switch to **Print Layout** view to see where the breaks are.

    »   **Tip**: Enable **Show/Hide** in the **Home** tab to view page break indicators.

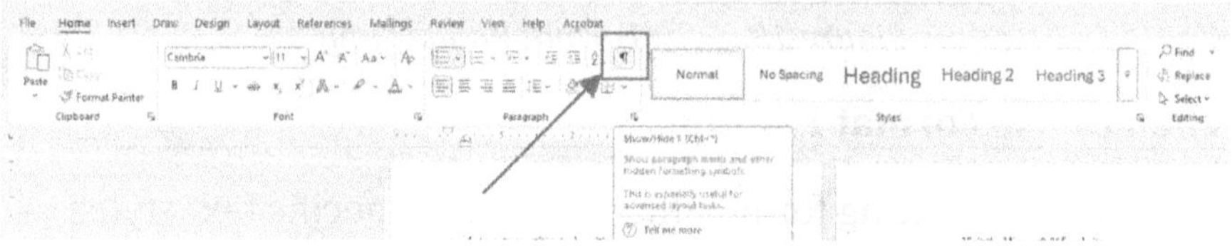

Figure 20.   Show Hide marks.png

2. Place your cursor directly before the page break line.
3. Press **Delete** (Windows) or **Backspace** (Mac).
4. The page break will be removed, merging the content into the previous page.

7. DELETING TEXT

Word provides several options for deleting text, whether it's a single character or an entire section.

Deleting a Single Character

*   Place your cursor to the left of the character and press **Delete**.
*   Alternatively, place your cursor to the right of the character and press **Backspace**.

Deleting Words

*   Hold down **Ctrl** (Windows) or **Option** (Mac) and press **Backspace** or **Delete** to remove one word at a time.

Deleting Sentences or Paragraphs

1. Select the sentence or paragraph you want to delete by dragging your mouse over it.
2. Press **Delete** or **Backspace** to remove the selection.

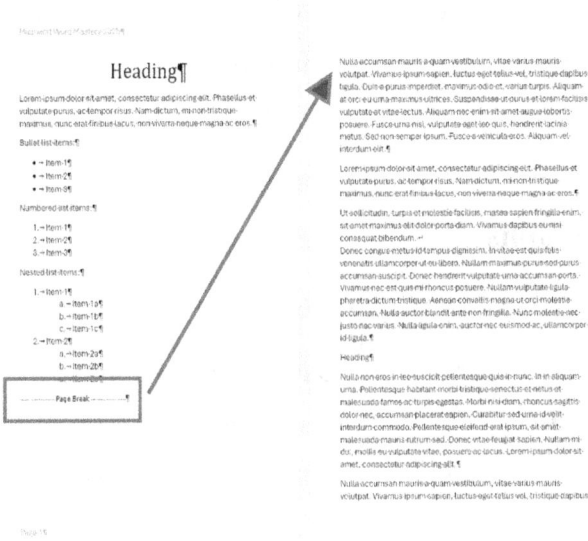

Deleting a Page

1. Go to the page you want to delete.

2. Highlight all the content on the page (use **Ctrl+A** or **Command+A** to select everything if needed).

3. Press **Delete** or **Backspace**.

    » **Tip**: Ensure there are no manual page breaks causing the empty page to remain.

II.   BASIC FORMATTING

1.   SPLIT AND JOIN PARAGRAPHS: MERGING AND SEPARATING IDEAS

Paragraphs in Word can be easily split or joined to help structure your content effectively, whether you're breaking ideas into smaller chunks or merging them for better flow.

Splitting Paragraphs

To separate a single paragraph into two:

1. Place your cursor where you want to create the split.
2. Press **Enter** to start a new paragraph from that point.
   » The text following the cursor will move to a new paragraph.

Joining Paragraphs

To combine two paragraphs into one:

1. Place your cursor at the end of the first paragraph.
2. Press **Backspace** or **Delete** to remove the paragraph break.
3. The second paragraph will merge with the first, continuing on the same line.

Tips for Effective Paragraph Management

- Split paragraphs to make text more readable and organized.
- Join paragraphs to combine closely related ideas or reduce unnecessary breaks.

2. SOFT AND HARD RETURNS: WHEN TO USE EACH

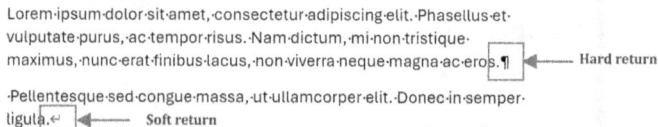

Figure 21.   Soft and Hard Returns.png

Returns determine how lines and paragraphs are spaced and structured in Word. Understanding the difference between soft and hard returns is key to creating a well-formatted document.

Hard Returns

- Created by pressing **Enter**.
- Signals the end of a paragraph and starts a new one.

- Use hard returns when you want a clear separation between paragraphs or sections.

Soft Returns

- Created by pressing **Shift+Enter**.
- Moves the cursor to the next line without starting a new paragraph.
- Use soft returns for breaking lines within the same paragraph, such as in an address or a poem.

When to Use Each

- **Hard Returns**: For separate paragraphs, headings, or lists.
- **Soft Returns**: For line breaks in titles, addresses, or structured content within a single paragraph.

Tip: Use the **Show/Hide Formatting Marks** (icon in the Home tab) to identify soft and hard returns in your document. Soft returns appear as arrows, and hard returns as paragraph symbols.

3. UNDO, REDO, AND REPEAT COMMANDS

Mistakes happen, and changes are sometimes necessary. Microsoft Word makes it easy to reverse, redo, or repeat actions with simple commands.

Undo

The Undo command reverses your last action:

- Use the keyboard shortcut **Ctrl+Z** (Windows) or **Command+Z** (Mac).
- Alternatively, click the **Undo** button (a curved arrow) on the Quick Access Toolbar.
- To undo multiple actions, click the Undo button repeatedly or click the dropdown arrow next to it to select specific actions to undo.

Redo

The Redo command reinstates the action you made before the Undo command:

- Use the keyboard shortcut **Ctrl+Y** (Windows) or **Command+Y** (Mac).
- Alternatively, click the **Redo** button (a curved arrow pointing in the opposite direction of Undo) on the Quick Access Toolbar.

Repeat

The Repeat command re-applies the last action you performed:

- Use the keyboard shortcut **F4** or **Ctrl+Y** (Windows) or **Command+Y** (Mac).

4. COPYING, CUTTING, AND PASTING CONTENT EFFICIENTLY

Moving or duplicating content is a frequent task in Word. These commands help you streamline the process.

Copying Content

The Copy command duplicates selected text or objects:

- Highlight the text or object you want to copy. Use the keyboard shortcut **Ctrl+C** (Windows) or **Command+C** (Mac).
- Alternatively, right-click the selection and choose **Copy** from the context menu.

Cutting Content

The Cut command removes selected content from its original location and places it on the clipboard:

- Highlight the text or object you want to cut. Use the keyboard shortcut **Ctrl+X** (Windows) or **Command+X** (Mac).

- Alternatively, right-click the selection and choose **Cut** from the context menu.

Pasting Content

The Paste command places the copied or cut content in a new location:

- Position the cursor where you want the content to appear. Use the keyboard shortcut **Ctrl+V** (Windows) or **Command+V** (Mac).
- Alternatively, right-click and choose **Paste** from the context menu.

Paste Options

Word offers additional options for how the content is inserted:

- **Keep Source Formatting**: Maintains the original font, size, and style.
- **Merge Formatting**: Adjusts the formatting to match the destination content.
- **Keep Text Only**: Strips all formatting and inserts plain text.

To access the paste option, right-click and choose Paste Options from the dialog.

Clipboard Manager

For multiple items, use the Clipboard Manager:

1. Go to the **Home** tab and click the small arrow in the Clipboard group.

Figure 22.   *Clipboard group.png*

2. Copy or cut multiple items, and the Clipboard will store them.

3. Select an item from the Clipboard pane to paste it into your document.

CHAPTER 3:

DOCUMENT FORMATTING

I.   FORMATTING WITH STYLES AND THEMES

Styles and themes are essential tools in Microsoft Word for creating documents that look polished and professional. By applying consistent formatting, you save time and ensure a cohesive design across your document.

1.   WHAT ARE STYLES?

Styles are predefined sets of formatting instructions that can be applied to text, paragraphs, or tables. They include font type, size, color, spacing, and alignment.

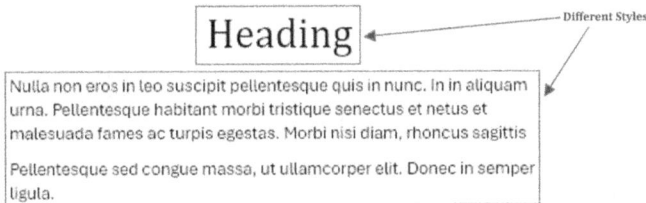

Heading — Different Styles

Nulla non eros in leo suscipit pellentesque quis in nunc. In in aliquam urna. Pellentesque habitant morbi tristique senectus et netus et malesuada fames ac turpis egestas. Morbi nisi diam, rhoncus sagittis

Pellentesque sed congue massa, ut ullamcorper elit. Donec in semper ligula.

Figure 23.   Styles.png

Using Built-in Styles

1.   Select the text or paragraph you want to format.

2.   Go to the **Home** tab and locate the **Styles** group.

3.   Click a style from the gallery, such as **Heading 1**, **Title**, or **Normal**.

Figure 24.   Word Styles.png

Modifying Styles

1. Right-click a style in the **Styles** gallery.

2. Select **Modify** to adjust font, size, alignment, or other attributes.

3. Click **OK** to save changes and apply the modified style.

Creating a Custom Style

1. Highlight text formatted with the attributes you want to save as a style.

2. In the **Styles** group, click the dropdown arrow and select **Create a Style**.

3. Name your style and click **OK**. The custom style will now appear in the **Styles** gallery.

2. WHAT ARE THEMES?

Themes are collections of fonts, colors, and effects that can be applied to an entire document for a unified look.

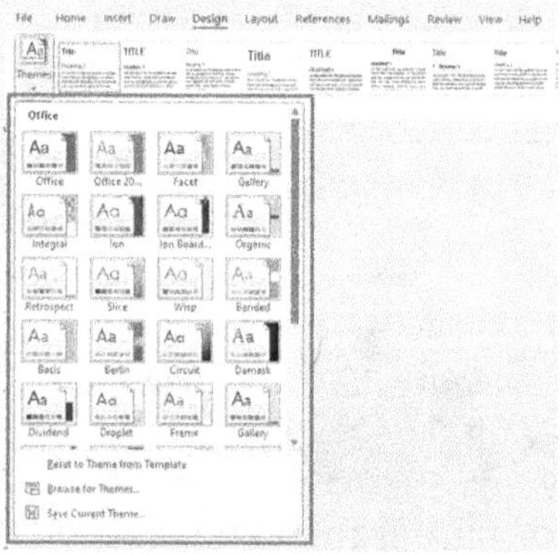

Figure 25.   *Themes.png*

Applying a Theme

1. Go to the **Design** tab and locate the **Themes** group.

2. Select a theme from the dropdown menu. The theme will adjust fonts, colors, and graphical effects throughout your document.

Customizing a Theme

1. In the **Design** tab, select **Colors** or **Fonts** to modify specific elements of the theme.

2. Choose **Set as Default** if you want the custom theme to be used for new documents.

3. BEST PRACTICES FOR USING STYLES AND THEMES

*   **Combine Styles with Themes**: Use styles for individual formatting and themes for overall design consistency.

*   **Plan Ahead**: Decide on styles and themes before starting your document to avoid repetitive adjustments.

*   **Keep It Simple**: Avoid overloading your document with many styles and themes, which creates a cluttered look.

II. SETTING PAPER SIZE, MARGINS, AND ORIENTATION FOR VARIOUS DOCUMENTS

Properly setting the paper size, margins, and orientation is crucial for ensuring your document meets professional or personal requirements. Microsoft Word makes it easy to customize these settings for any project.

1. SETTING PAPER SIZE

The paper size determines the dimensions of your document.

Standard sizes include Letter (8.5 x 11 inches) and A4 (8.27 x 11.69 inches).

Accessing Paper Size Settings:

1. Go to the **Layout** tab and click **Size** in the **Page Setup** group.

2. Select a preset size from the dropdown menu (e.g., Letter, A4, Legal).

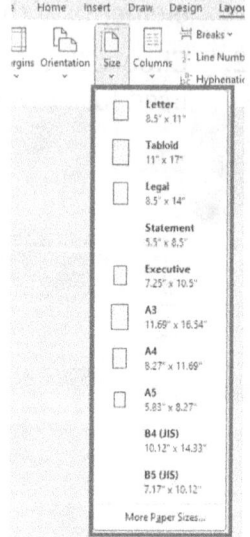

Customizing Paper Size:

1. Click **More Paper Sizes** at the bottom of the **Size** dropdown.

2. In the dialog box, input custom width and height dimensions.

3. Click **OK** to apply.

2. ADJUSTING MARGINS

Margins are the blank spaces between your content and the edges of the page. Adjusting them can optimize your document's layout and readability.

Using Preset Margins:

1. Go to the **Layout** tab, click **Margins** in the **Page Setup** group.

2. Choose from presets like **Normal**, **Narrow**, **Wide**, or **Custom Margins**.

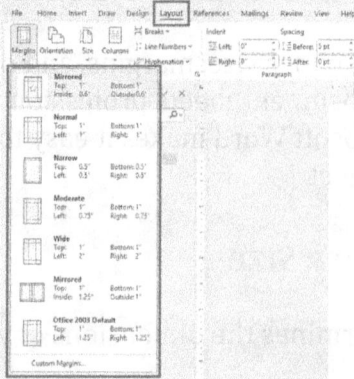

Customizing Margins:

1. Select **Custom Margins** from the **Margins** dropdown.

2. In the **Page Setup** dialog box, input specific values for top, bottom, left, and right margins.

3. Click **OK** to save changes.

3. CHOOSING PAGE ORIENTATION

Orientation determines whether your document is displayed vertically (Portrait) or horizontally (Landscape).

Changing Orientation:

1. Go to the **Layout** tab and click **Orientation** in the **Page Setup** group.

2. Select either **Portrait** or **Landscape**.

When to Use Each Orientation:

*   **Portrait**: Best for text-heavy documents like letters, essays, or reports.

*   **Landscape**: Ideal for charts, graphs, or wide tables.

4. TIPS FOR SETTING UP YOUR DOCUMENT LAYOUT

*   **Check Printing Requirements**: Ensure your paper size and margins match the specifications of your printer.

*   **Preview Your Layout**: Use **File > Print** to view how your document will appear when printed.

*   **Use Consistent Settings**: For multi-section documents, ensure the layout settings are consistent throughout.

III. USING SECTION BREAKS FOR ADVANCED LAYOUT

Section breaks allow you to organize and structure your document effectively. They help you manage complex layouts, control content flow, and apply different formatting to specific parts of your document.

Types of Section Breaks

- **Next Page**: Starts a new section on the next page.
- **Continuous**: Starts a new section on the same page.
- **Even Page**: Begins a new section on the next even-numbered page.
- **Odd Page**: Begins a new section on the next odd-numbered page.

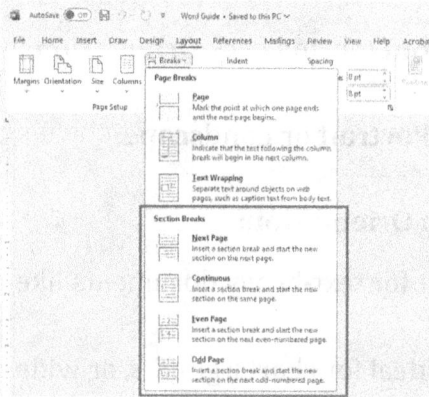

Figure 26.   *Section Break.png*

Inserting Section Breaks

1. Place your cursor where you want to insert the break.
2. Go to the **Layout** tab, click **Breaks**, and choose the desired section break.

Removing Section Breaks

1. Enable **Show/Hide Formatting Marks** in the **Home** tab to see section breaks.
2. Highlight the section break and press **Delete** or **Backspace**.

Practical Uses for Section Breaks

- **Different Headers and Footers**: Use section breaks to apply unique headers and footers.

- **Page Orientation**: Change part of your document to landscape while keeping the rest in portrait orientation.

- **Columns**: Apply multi-column formatting to specific sections without affecting the entire document.

IV.   ADDING HEADERS, FOOTERS, AND PAGE NUMBERS

Headers, footers, and page numbers are essential elements in creating well-organized and professional documents. They provide context and navigation for readers while maintaining a consistent layout.

1.   ADDING HEADERS AND FOOTERS

Headers appear at the top of each page, while footers are placed at the bottom. Both can include text, graphics, or dynamic elements like page numbers and dates.

Inserting a Header or Footer

1. Go to the **Insert** tab and click **Header** or **Footer** in the **Header & Footer** group.

2. Choose a style from the dropdown menu or select **Edit Header/Edit Footer** to create a custom design.

3. Type your content in the header or footer area, such as a title, date, or company logo.

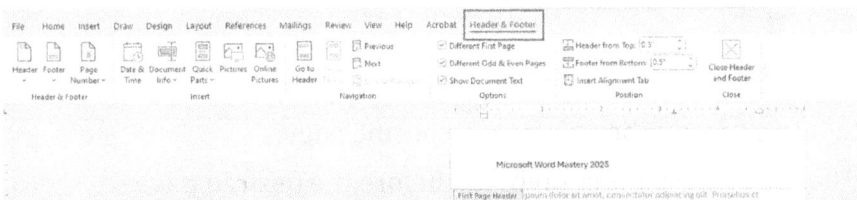

Figure 27.   *Header and Footer Edit.png*

Customizing Headers and Footers

1. Use the **Header & Footer Tools** tab to:
   - » Align content left, center, or right.
   - » Insert images, text, or additional elements like dates.
   - » Format text using font styles and sizes.

2. To apply different headers or footers to specific sections:
   - » Insert a section break (see previous section).
   - » Uncheck **Link to Previous** in the **Header & Footer Tools** tab.

2. ADDING PAGE NUMBERS

Page numbers make it easier to navigate long documents and reference specific sections.

Inserting Page Numbers

1. Go to the **Insert** tab and click **Page Number** in the **Header & Footer** group.

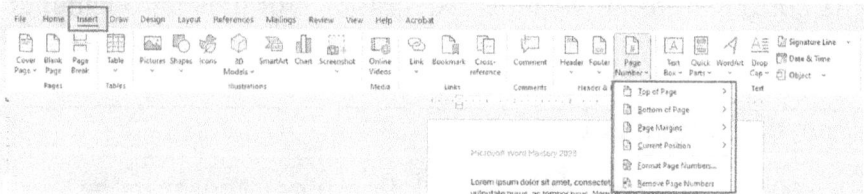

Figure 28.   **Insert Page Number.png**

2. Choose a location (Top of Page, Bottom of Page, or Page Margins) and select a style.
3. The page numbers will appear automatically in the chosen position.

Customizing Page Numbers

1. To start numbering from a specific page:
   - » Insert a section break before the desired page.

- » Go to **Insert > Page Number > Format Page Numbers**, and set the starting number.
2. To format page numbers:
   - » Select **Format Page Numbers** from the **Page Number** dropdown.
   - » Choose a number format (e.g., Roman numerals or alphabetical).
3. To remove page numbers from specific sections:
   - » Use a section break to isolate the section.
   - » Uncheck **Link to Previous** in the header or footer area and delete the page number.

3. TIPS FOR HEADERS, FOOTERS, AND PAGE NUMBERS

- **Preview Your Changes**: Use the **Print Layout** view to see how headers, footers, and page numbers appear.
- **Avoid Clutter**: Keep headers and footers simple for readability and professionalism.
- **Use Dynamic Fields**: Add dynamic elements like the document title or current date by clicking **Quick Parts > Field** in the **Header & Footer Tools** tab.

V.   INSERTING AUTOMATIC TABLE OF CONTENTS

An automatic table of contents (TOC) provides a structured overview of your document, making it easier for readers to navigate. Word allows you to generate a TOC automatically based on the headings in your document.

1. INSERTING A TABLE OF CONTENTS

Preparing Your Document for a Table of Contents

Before inserting a TOC, ensure your document is properly structured:

1. Use **Heading Styles** for section titles:
   » Highlight the section title.
   » Go to the **Home** tab and select a heading style (e.g., **Heading 1**, **Heading 2**) from the **Styles** group.

2. Apply consistent heading levels throughout your document for clear organization.

Inserting a Table of Contents

1. Place your cursor where you want the TOC to appear (typically at the beginning of the document).

2. Go to the **References** tab and click **Table of Contents** in the **Table of Contents** group.

3. Choose a built-in TOC style from the dropdown menu (e.g., Classic, Modern, or Formal).

4. Word will automatically generate a TOC based on your headings.

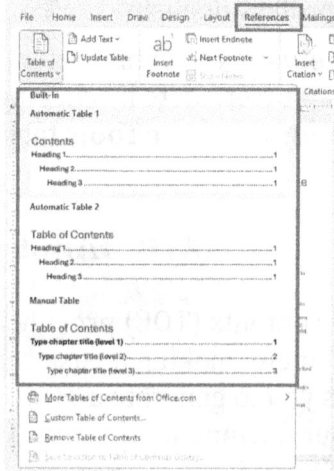

Figure 29.   *CreateTOC.png*

2. UPDATING AND CUSTOMIZING TABLE OF CONTENTS

Updating the Table of Contents

As you make changes to your document, the TOC does not update automatically. Here's how to refresh it:

1. Click anywhere inside the TOC.

2. Select **Update Table** in the upper-left corner of the TOC.

3. Choose either:

- **Update page numbers only**: If you've made no structural changes but content has shifted.

- **Update entire table**: If you've added, removed, or renamed headings.

Customizing the Table of Contents

1. Go to **References > Table of Contents > Custom Table of Contents**.

2. In the dialog box, adjust the following:

   » **Show Levels**: Choose how many heading levels to include.

   » **Tab Leader**: Select dots, dashes, or no leader for the TOC.

   » **Formats**: Choose from pre-defined TOC designs or create a custom style.

3. Click **OK** to apply the changes.

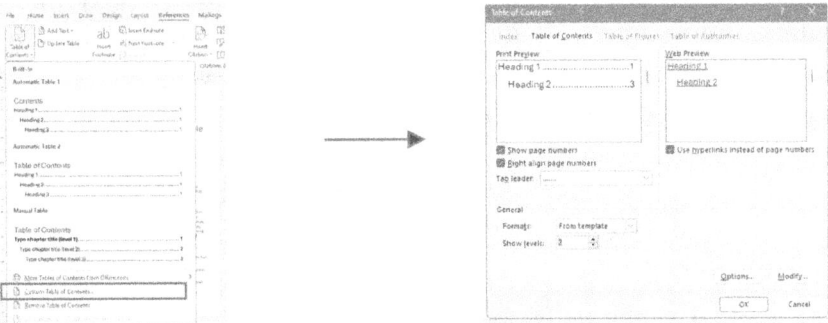

Figure 30.   *Customize TOC.png*

Removing the Table of Contents

If you need to remove the TOC:

1. Click inside the TOC.
2. Go to **References > Table of Contents > Remove Table of Contents**.

3. TIPS FOR A CLEAR TABLE OF CONTENTS

- **Use Descriptive Headings**: Ensure each section title clearly represents the content it covers.

- **Keep It Simple**: Avoid overloading the TOC with too many levels to maintain readability.

- **Preview Before Printing**: Check the TOC in **Print Layout** view to ensure accuracy and proper alignment.

VI.   ADDING CAPTIONS AND INSERTING AUTOMATIC TABLE OF FIGURES

Captions and an automatic Table of Figures are essential for organizing and referencing visual elements like images, charts, and tables in your document. They make your content more accessible and professional.

1. ADDING CAPTIONS TO FIGURES

Captions provide a short description for visual elements, helping readers understand their context.

Steps to Add a Caption

1. Select the figure (image, chart, or table) you want to caption.
2. Go to the **References** tab and click **Insert Caption** in the **Captions** group.
3. In the dialog box:
   » Enter the caption text (e.g., "Figure 1: Sales Trends for 2025").
   » Choose the label type (e.g., **Figure**, **Table**, or **Equation**).
   » Select the position (**Above Selected Item** or **Below**

Selected Item).

4. Click **OK** to insert the caption.

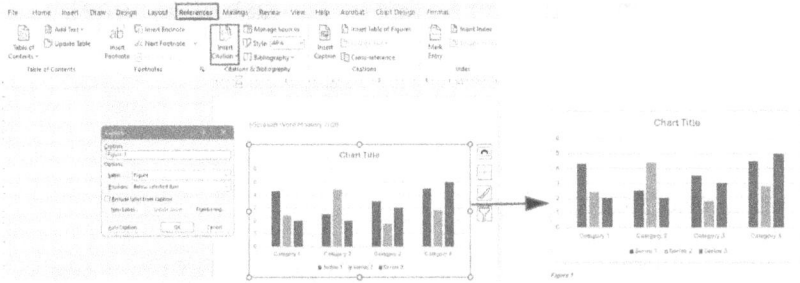

Customizing Caption Labels

1. In the **Insert Caption** dialog box, click **New Label** to create a custom label. Example: Replace "Figure" with "Image" or "Chart."

2. Use consistent labels throughout your document for clarity.

2. CREATING AN AUTOMATIC TABLE OF FIGURES

A Table of Figures is a list of all the captions in your document, similar to a Table of Contents. It helps readers quickly locate visual elements.

Steps to Insert a Table of Figures

1. Place your cursor where you want the Table of Figures to appear (typically after the Table of Contents).

2. Go to the **References** tab and click **Insert Table of Figures** in the **Captions** group.

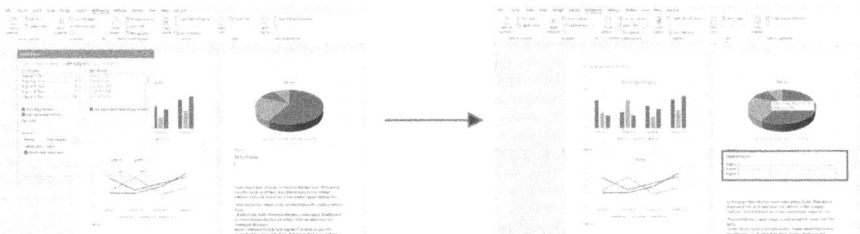

Figure 31.   *Insert Table of Figures.png*

3. In the dialog box:
   - » Choose the caption label to include (e.g., **Figure**, **Table**).
   - » Customize the tab leader (dots, dashes, or none).
   - » Adjust formatting options as needed.
4. Click **OK** to generate the Table of Figures.

Updating the Table of Figures

1. After adding or modifying captions, click inside the Table of Figures.
2. Click **Update Table** in the upper-left corner of the table.
3. Choose **Update page numbers only** or **Update entire table**, depending on your changes.

3. BEST PRACTICES FOR CAPTIONS AND TABLES OF FIGURES

- **Be Consistent**: Use the same label style and formatting for all captions.
- **Keep Captions Concise**: Provide just enough detail to describe the visual element.
- **Preview Layout**: Check the Table of Figures in **Print Layout** view to ensure proper alignment and readability.

VII. DESIGNING A COVER PAGE

A well-designed cover page sets the tone for your document and provides essential information such as the title, author, and date. Microsoft Word offers built-in tools and templates to create professional and visually appealing cover pages with ease.

1. USING BUILT-IN COVER PAGE TEMPLATES

Word includes a variety of pre-designed cover page templates that you can customize to suit your document's needs.

Steps to Insert a Cover Page

1. Go to the **Insert** tab and click **Cover Page**.

2. Select a template from the dropdown menu. Templates include placeholders for text, images, and other elements.

3. Click on the placeholders and replace the sample text with your own content (e.g., document title, author name, and date).

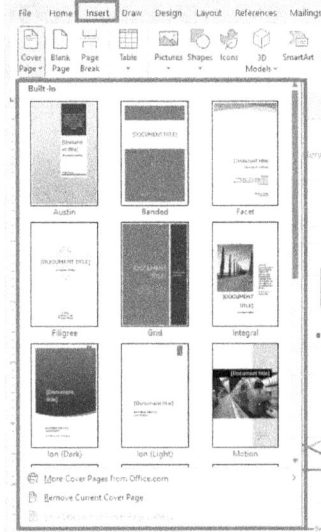

2. CUSTOMIZING A COVER PAGE

To make the cover page unique and tailored to your needs, you can modify or create your own design.

Modify a Template

After inserting a template, customize it by:

- Changing fonts, colors, and sizes using the **Home** tab.

- Adding your company logo or other images using the **Insert > Pictures** option.

- Adjusting layout elements by dragging and resizing text boxes or images.

Creating a Custom Cover Page

1. Start with a blank page by inserting a **Blank Page** from the **Insert** tab.

2. Use the following tools to design your cover page:

   » **Text Boxes**: Go to **Insert > Text Box** to add titles, subtitles, or author names.

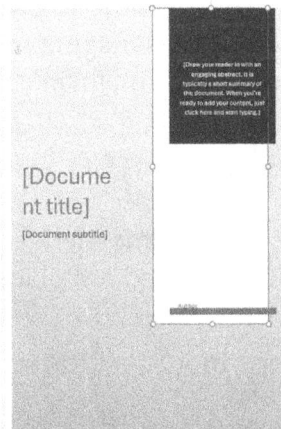

- » **Shapes**: Use **Insert > Shapes** to add decorative elements like lines or rectangles.
- » **Pictures**: Insert images or logos to enhance the visual appeal.
- » **Themes**: Apply a theme from the **Design** tab for consistent formatting.

3. Once the design is complete, save it as a template:
   - » Highlight all elements on the cover page.
   - » Go to **File > Save As** and choose **Word Template** as the file format.

3. TIPS FOR AN EFFECTIVE COVER PAGE

- **Keep It Simple**: Avoid clutter by including only essential information.
- **Align with Your Document's Purpose**: Use fonts, colors, and images that match the tone of your document (e.g., professional for reports, creative for event programs).
- **Maintain Consistency**: Ensure the cover page design aligns with the rest of your document's theme and style.

VIII. WORKING WITH CITATIONS AND REFERENCES

Citations and references are essential for academic, professional, and research-based documents. Microsoft Word simplifies the process of managing sources and creating bibliographies, ensuring proper citation formatting.

1. ADDING CITATIONS

Citations acknowledge the sources of information used in your document and are placed where the reference is made.

Steps to Add a Citation

1. Go to the **References** tab and click **Insert Citation** in the

Citations & Bibliography group.

2. Select **Add New Source** from the dropdown.

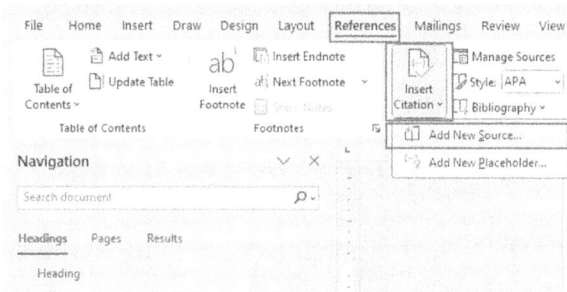

Figure 32. **Insert Citation.png**

3. In the **Create Source** dialog box:

» Choose the source type (e.g., book, journal, website).

» Fill in the required details (author, title, year, etc.).

» Click OK to save the source.

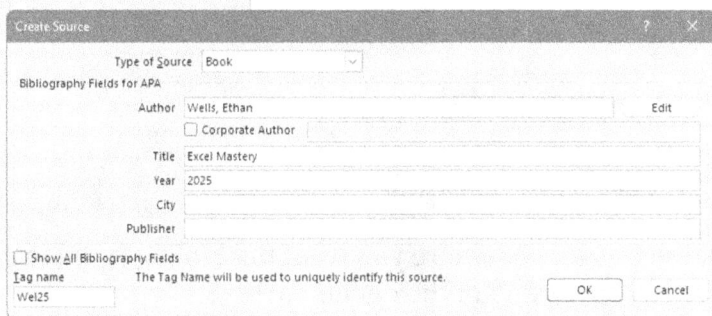

4. The citation will be inserted in the selected format (e.g., APA, MLA).

2. MANAGING SOURCES

The **Source Manager** allows you to organize and reuse citations across documents.

1. Click **Manage Sources** in the **Citations & Bibliography** group.

2. In the dialog box:

   » View all sources in the **Current List** or **Master List**.

   » Edit or delete existing sources as needed.

   » Copy sources between the lists for use in different documents.

3. CREATING A BIBLIOGRAPHY OR WORKS CITED PAGE

A bibliography or works cited page is a list of all the sources cited in your document.

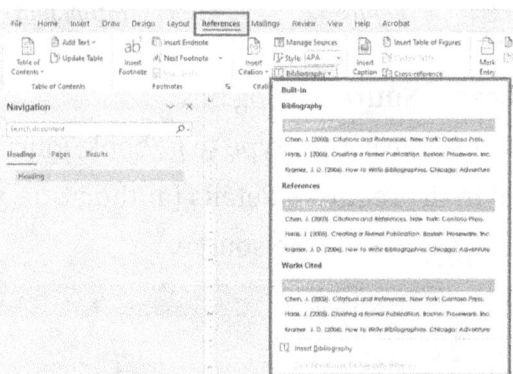

Figure 33.   ***Bibliography.png***

Steps to Insert a Bibliography

1. Place your cursor where you want the bibliography to appear (usually at the end of the document).

2. Go to the **References** tab and click **Bibliography** in the **Citations & Bibliography** group.

3. Choose a built-in bibliography or works cited style from the dropdown.

4. FORMATTING CITATIONS AND BIBLIOGRAPHIES

Word supports various citation styles, including APA, MLA, and Chicago.

Changing the Citation Style

1. Go to the **References** tab and select a style from the **Style** dropdown in the **Citations & Bibliography** group.
2. Word will automatically update all citations and the bibliography to match the selected style.

Customizing the Appearance

1. Highlight the citation or bibliography text.
2. Use the formatting tools in the **Home** tab to adjust font, size, or spacing.

5. USING CROSS-REFERENCES

Cross-references link to specific elements within the document, such as tables, figures, or headings.

Steps to Add a Cross-Reference

1. Place your cursor where you want the reference to appear.
2. Go to the **References** tab and click **Cross-reference**.
3. Select the type of reference (e.g., heading, figure, table).
4. Choose the specific item from the list and click **Insert**.

6. TIPS FOR WORKING WITH CITATIONS AND REFERENCES

- **Keep Your Sources Organized**: Use the Source Manager to maintain a master list of frequently used references.
- **Double-Check Accuracy**: Ensure that the citation style and source details meet the required guidelines.
- **Use Cross-References for Navigation**: Link to figures, tables, or sections for easier navigation in long documents.

CHAPTER 4:

BORDERS AND TABLES

I.   BORDERS

Borders are an excellent way to add structure, emphasis, or a decorative touch to your document. You can apply borders to text, paragraphs, or entire pages in Microsoft Word.

1.   ADDING BORDERS TO TEXT

Text borders highlight specific content, such as headings or important notes.

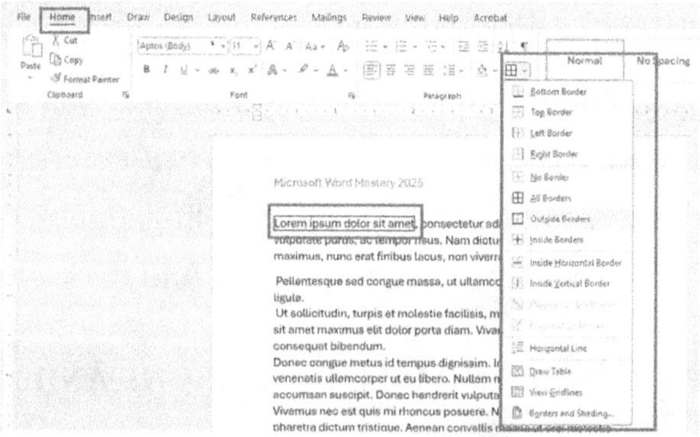

Figure 34.   *Text border.png*

Steps to Add a Text Border

1. Select the text you want to surround with a border.
2. Go to the **Home** tab and click the **Borders** dropdown in the **Paragraph** group.
3. Choose a border style (e.g., Bottom Border, All Borders).
4. To customize the border:
    »   Select **Borders and Shading** from the dropdown.

- » In the dialog box, choose the border style, color, and width.
- » Click **OK** to apply the changes.

2. ADDING BORDERS TO PARAGRAPHS

Borders around paragraphs can visually separate blocks of text or emphasize key sections.

Steps to Add a Paragraph Border

1. Place your cursor inside the paragraph or select multiple paragraphs.
2. Go to the **Home** tab and open the **Borders** dropdown.
3. Choose **Borders and Shading** for more options.
4. In the dialog box: Under **Settings**, select the desired border type (e.g., Box, Shadow, or Custom).
   - » Adjust border style, color, and width.
5. Click **OK** to apply.

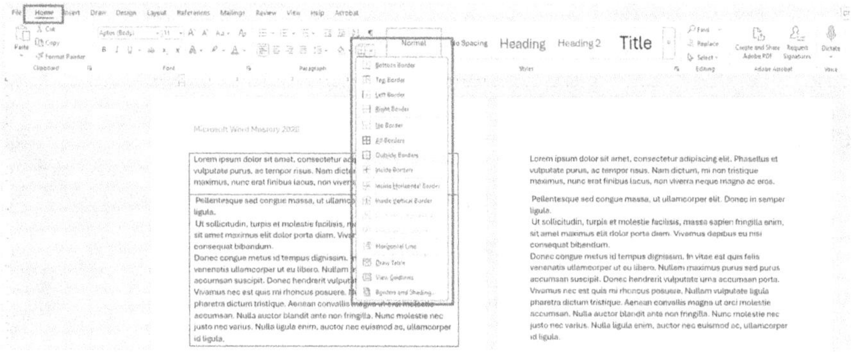

Figure 35.   *Paragraph border.png*

3. ADDING PAGE BORDERS

Page borders are ideal for adding a decorative or professional frame around the entire page.

Steps to Add a Page Border

1. Go to the **Design** tab and click **Page Borders** in the **Page Background** group.

2. In the **Borders and Shading** dialog box:

    » Under **Settings**, choose **Box**, **Shadow**, or **3D**.

    » Select the desired border style, color, and width. To use a decorative design, choose an option from the **Art** dropdown.

3. Under **Apply To**, select where the border should appear on.

4. Click **OK** to apply the border.

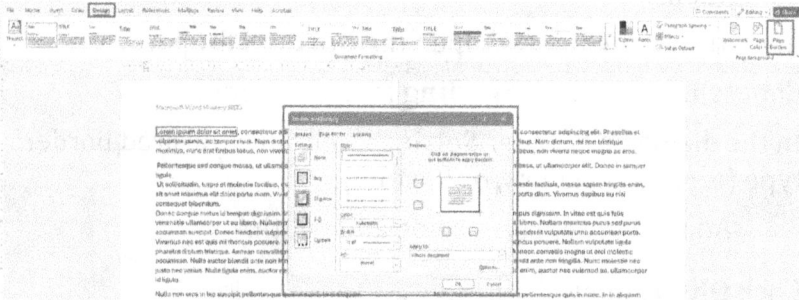

Figure 36.   Page Border.png

4. REMOVING BORDERS

To remove unwanted borders:

5. Select the text, paragraph, or page with the border.

6. Open the **Borders** dropdown in the **Home** tab.

7. Select **No Border** to remove the applied border.

5. TIPS FOR USING BORDERS EFFECTIVELY

-   **Keep It Simple**: Use subtle borders for professional documents and bold ones for creative or informal projects.

-   **Combine with Shading**: Pair borders with background shading for added emphasis (found in the **Borders and Shading** dialog box).

-   **Preview Before Finalizing**: Use the **Print Preview** feature to ensure borders align well with your document's layout.

II. CREATING AND FORMATTING TABLES FOR STRUCTURED DATA

Tables are an effective way to organize and present structured data in your document. Microsoft Word provides robust tools to create and customize tables for various purposes, from simple layouts to complex data presentations.

1. CREATING A TABLE

Using the Table Grid

1. Go to the **Insert** tab and click **Table** in the **Tables** group.
2. Hover over the grid to select the desired number of rows and columns.
3. Click to insert the table into your document.

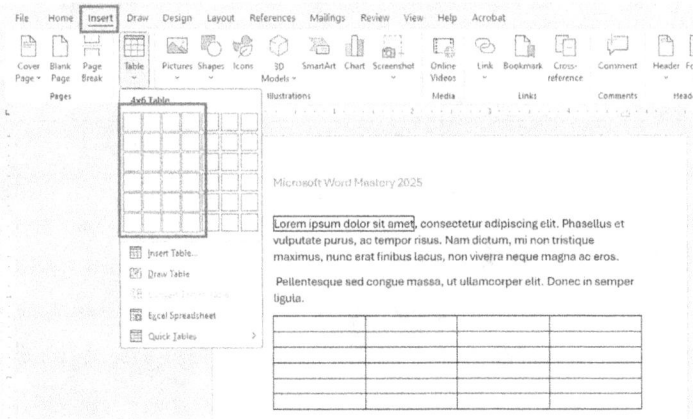

Figure 37.   Using Table Grid.png

Using the Insert Table Option

1. Go to the **Insert** tab and click **Table**.
2. Select **Insert Table** from the dropdown menu.
3. Specify the number of rows and columns in the dialog box.

4. Click **OK** to insert the table.

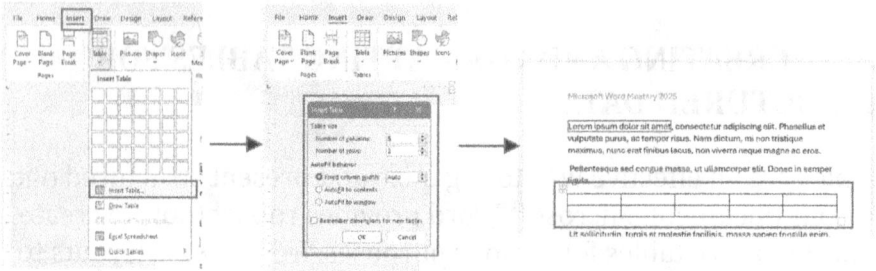

Figure 38.   Using Insert Table Option.png

Drawing a Custom Table

1. Go to the **Insert** tab and click **Table**.
2. Select **Draw Table** from the dropdown menu.
3. Use the pencil tool to draw the table's borders manually. Click and drag to create cells, rows, or columns.

Figure 39.   Using Draw Table.png

2. FORMATTING TABLES

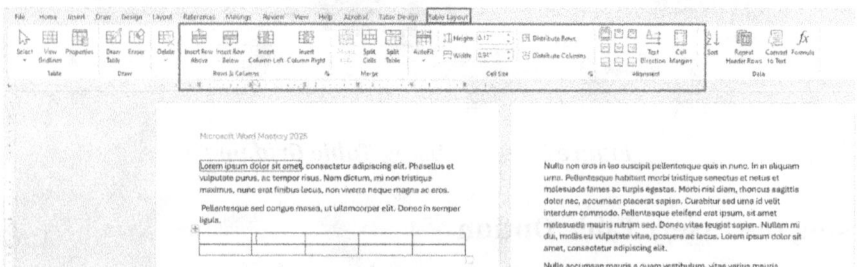

Figure 40.   Customize Table.png

Adjusting Table Dimensions

1. Hover over a table border until you see the resize cursor (a double arrow). Drag the border to adjust row height or column width.
2. Alternatively, go to the **Layout** tab (under **Table Tools**) and use the **Height** and **Width** options to set precise dimensions.

Applying Table Styles

1. Click anywhere in the table.
2. Go to the **Table Design** tab (under **Table Tools**).
3. Choose a style from the **Table Styles** gallery for quick formatting.
4. Customize the style by selecting options like **Header Row**, **Banded Rows**, or **First Column** in the **Table Style Options** group.

Shading and Borders

1. Select the cells, rows, or columns you want to format.
2. Go to the **Table Design** tab:
   » Use **Shading** to add background color.
   » Use **Borders** to adjust the style, color, and width of cell borders.

Aligning Text in Cells

1. Select the cells you want to align.
2. Go to the **Layout** tab (under **Table Tools**) and use the **Alignment** group to choose text alignment (e.g., Top Left, Center, or Bottom Right).

Adding Rows or Columns

1. Click inside the table near where you want to add rows or columns.
2. Go to the **Layout** tab (under **Table Tools**) and use the options in the **Rows & Columns** group:

> » **Insert Above** or **Insert Below** for rows.
>
> » **Insert Left** or **Insert Right** for columns.

Deleting Rows or Columns

1. Select the rows or columns you want to remove.
2. Go to the **Layout** tab and click **Delete** in the **Rows & Columns** group.
3. Choose **Delete Rows**, **Delete Columns**, or **Delete Table** as needed.

Merging Cells

1. Select the cells you want to merge.
2. Go to the **Layout** tab and click **Merge Cells** in the **Merge** group.

Splitting Cells

1. Select the cell you want to split.
2. Go to the **Layout** tab and click **Split Cells** in the **Merge** group.
3. Specify the number of rows and columns for the split.

3. TIPS FOR USING TABLES EFFECTIVELY

- **Plan Your Layout**: Determine the number of rows and columns needed before creating a table.
- **Use Simple Styles**: Keep formatting clean and readable for professional documents.
- **Preview Before Printing**: Check how the table appears in **Print Layout** to ensure alignment and spacing.

III. PLACING A COLUMN BREAK: MANAGING MULTI-COLUMN LAYOUTS

Multi-column layouts are a powerful way to format documents

such as newsletters, brochures, and reports. Column breaks allow you to control the flow of content between columns, ensuring a polished and organized layout.

1. CREATING A MULTI-COLUMN LAYOUT

Steps to Add Columns

1. Go to the **Layout** tab.
2. Click **Columns** in the **Page Setup** group.
3. Choose a preset option:
   - » **One**: Standard single-column layout.
   - » **Two** or **Three**: Splits content into the selected number of columns.
   - » **Left** or **Right**: Creates one narrow and one wide column.
4. If none of the presets fit your needs, select **More Columns** to customize the width and spacing of each column.

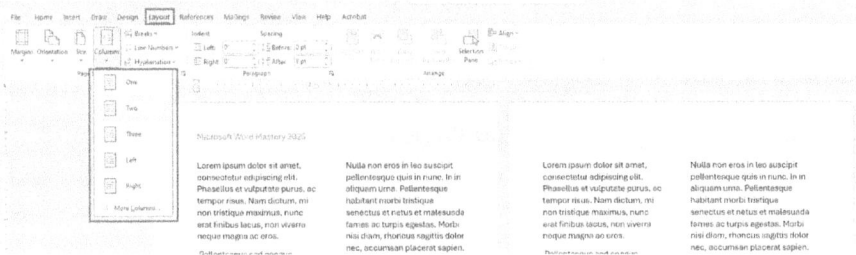

Figure 41.   *Create Columns.png*

Balancing Column Lengths

To balance the content across columns, insert a column break where necessary (explained below).

2. PLACING A COLUMN BREAK

Column breaks move content from one column to the next, giving you precise control over text placement.

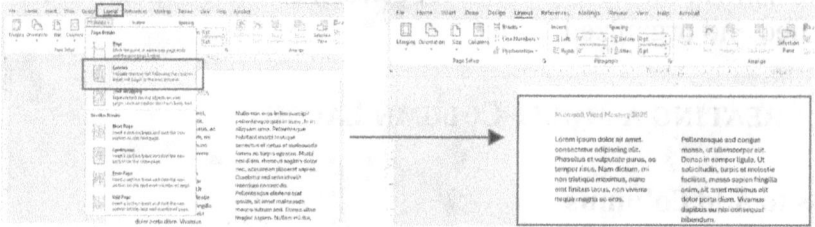

Figure 42. **Insert Column Break.png**

Steps to Insert a Column Break

1. Place your cursor where you want the content to move to the next column.

2. Go to the **Layout** tab.

3. Click **Breaks** in the **Page Setup** group.

4. Select **Column** from the dropdown menu. The text after the break will move to the next column.

3. CUSTOMIZING COLUMNS

Adjusting Column Width and Spacing

1. Go to the **Layout** tab and click **Columns** > **More Columns**.

2. In the dialog box:
   » Adjust the width of each column.
   » Modify the spacing between columns.
   » Check **Line Between** to add a vertical line between the columns.

3. Click **OK** to apply the changes.

Applying Columns to Specific Sections

1. Highlight the text you want to format into columns.

2. Go to the **Layout** tab and click **Columns**.

3. Choose the desired column layout. Only the selected text will be formatted, leaving the rest of the document unchanged.

Removing Columns

1. Highlight the content formatted into columns.

2. Go to the **Layout** tab and click **Columns**.

3. Select **One** to revert to a single-column layout.

IV.   GRAPHICAL WORKS IN MICROSOFT WORD

Visual elements like shapes, images, icons, and SmartArt enhance the impact and clarity of your documents. Microsoft Word provides tools to insert and customize these elements, making your documents more engaging and visually appealing.

1.   INSERTING AND CUSTOMIZING SHAPES, IMAGES, AND ICONS

Figure 43.   Insert Pictures, Shapes and Icons.png

Adding Shapes

Shapes can highlight important information or create visual interest.

1. Go to the **Insert** tab and click **Shapes** in the **Illustrations** group.

2. Select a shape (e.g., rectangle, arrow, circle) from the dropdown menu.

3. Click and drag on the document to draw the shape.

Customizing Shapes

1. Select the shape to open the **Shape Format** tab.

2. Use the following tools:

    » **Fill**: Change the shape's color with **Shape Fill**.

- » **Outline**: Adjust the color, thickness, or style of the border with **Shape Outline**.
- » **Effects**: Add shadows, reflections, or 3D effects using **Shape Effects**.

3. Resize the shape by dragging its edges or corners.

Inserting Images

Images help convey information more effectively and add visual appeal.

1. Go to the **Insert** tab and click **Pictures** in the **Illustrations** group.

2. Choose **This Device** to upload an image from your computer or **Online Pictures** to search for web-based images.

3. Select the image and click **Insert** to add it to your document.

Customizing Images

1. Select the image to open the **Picture Format** tab.

2. Use tools like:
   - » **Crop**: Trim unnecessary parts of the image.
   - » **Corrections**: Adjust brightness, contrast, or sharpness.
   - » **Picture Styles**: Add frames, borders, or effects to your image.

Inserting Icons

Icons are modern, scalable graphics that work well for visual communication.

1. Go to the **Insert** tab, click **Icons** in the **Illustrations** group.

2. Browse or search for an icon from Word's library.

3. Select an icon and click **Insert**.

4. Customize the icon's size, color, or position using the **Graphics Format** tab.

2. USING SMARTART FOR VISUAL HIERARCHY

SmartArt provides pre-designed diagrams to visually represent relationships, processes, or hierarchies.

Inserting SmartArt

1. Go to the **Insert** tab and click **SmartArt** in the **Illustrations** group.

2. Choose a category (e.g., List, Process, Cycle, Hierarchy).

3. Select a layout and click **OK**.

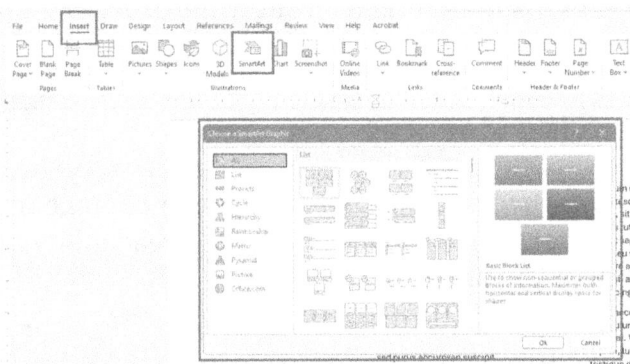

Figure 44.   Insert SmartArt.png

Customizing SmartArt

1. Click inside the SmartArt graphic to add text.

2. Use the **SmartArt Design** tab to customize:

   » **Styles**: Apply pre-set styles for 3D effects, shadows, or outlines.

   » **Colors**: Change the color scheme to match your document's theme.

3. Resize or rearrange elements within the diagram by dragging or using the **Promote/Demote** options.

CHAPTER 5:

ADVANCED LAYOUT & DESIGN

I.   PAGE SETUPS FOR PRINTING

Proper page setup is critical for creating print-ready documents that meet professional standards. Microsoft Word offers tools to adjust margins, paper size, and layout while providing a preview to ensure everything looks perfect before printing.

1.   ADJUSTING MARGINS

Margins define the blank space between your content and the edges of the page. Correct margins improve readability and give your document a polished look.

Setting Margins

1. Go to the **Layout** tab and click **Margins** in the **Page Setup** group.

2. Select a preset option (e.g., Normal, Narrow, Wide) from the dropdown menu.

3. For custom margins:

   » Click **Custom Margins** at the bottom of the dropdown.

   » In the dialog box, specify the values for top, bottom, left, and right margins.

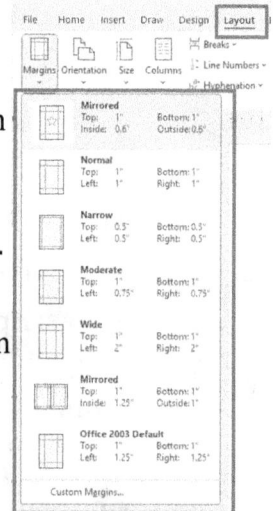

   » Click **OK** to apply.

Tips for Margins

• Use **Normal (1-inch margins)** for standard documents like essays or reports.

- Adjust margins for special documents (e.g., Narrow margins for flyers or Wide margins for formal letters).

2. SELECTING PAPER SIZE

Choosing the correct paper size ensures your document prints correctly on the intended medium.

Steps to Change Paper Size

1. Go to the **Layout** tab and click **Size** in the **Page Setup** group.

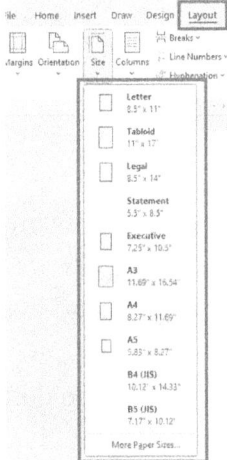

2. Select a preset size (e.g., Letter, Legal, A4) from the dropdown menu.
3. For custom sizes:
   » Click **More Paper Sizes** at the bottom of the dropdown.
   » Specify the width and height in the dialog box.
   » Click **OK** to apply.

Tips for Paper Size

- Use **Letter (8.5 x 11 inches)** for most standard documents.
- Choose **A4 (8.27 x 11.69 inches)** for international printing.

3. PAGE ORIENTATION

Orientation determines whether your document is displayed vertically (Portrait) or horizontally (Landscape).

Changing Orientation

1. Go to the **Layout** tab and click **Orientation** in the **Page Setup** group.
2. Choose **Portrait** (default) or **Landscape** to adjust the layout.

4. PREVIEWING YOUR DOCUMENT BEFORE PRINTING

Previewing ensures your document looks as intended before sending it to the printer.

Steps to Preview

1. Go to **File > Print** to open the Print Preview screen.
2. Review the layout, margins, and overall formatting.
3. Use the zoom slider to examine details like alignment and spacing.

Making Adjustments from Print Preview

- If something doesn't look right, click **Back** to return to your document and make changes.
- Revisit the **Layout** tab to adjust margins, paper size, or orientation.

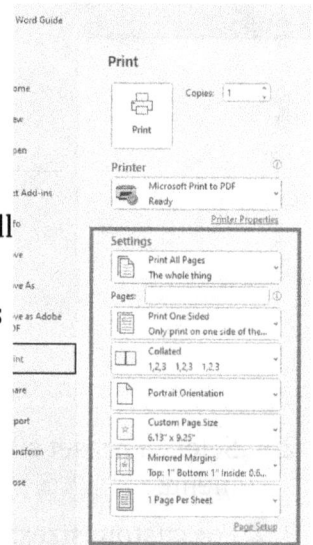

II. ALIGNING AND POSITIONING OBJECTS WITH PRECISION

Precise alignment and positioning of objects like text boxes, images, and shapes are essential for creating professional and visually appealing documents. Microsoft Word provides tools to ensure your layouts are polished and well-organized.

1. ALIGNING OBJECTS

Using the Align Tool

1. Select the object(s) you want to align.

2. Go to the **Shape Format** or **Picture Format** tab (depending on the type of object).

3. Click **Align** in the **Arrange** group.

4. Choose an alignment option:

   » **Align Left**: Aligns objects to the left margin.

   » **Align Center**: Centers objects horizontally.

   » **Align Right**: Aligns objects to the right margin.

   » **Align Top, Middle, Bottom**: Aligns objects vertically relative to the page or other objects.

   » **Distribute Horizontally** or **Distribute Vertically:** Aligns objects evenly. These options only appear if you select at least 3 objects.

Figure 45.   Align objects.png

Using Grids and Guides

Grids and guides help position objects accurately on the page.

- **Turning On Grids and Guides**
  - » Go to the **View** tab.
  - » Check **Gridlines** or **Guides** in the **Show** group.

- **Customizing Grid Settings**
  - » Go to **File > Options > Advanced** and scroll to the **Display** section.
  - » Adjust grid spacing or enable **Snap objects to grid when the gridlines are not displayed** for precise placement.

2. POSITIONING OBJECTS

Wrapping Text Around Objects

1. Select the object.
2. Go to the **Picture Format** or **Shape Format** tab and click **Wrap Text** in the **Arrange** group.
3. Choose a text-wrapping option:
   - » **Square**: Text flows around the object in a square pattern.
   - » **Tight**: Text closely follows the shape of the object.
   - » **Behind Text** or **In Front of Text**: Places the object behind or in front of the text.

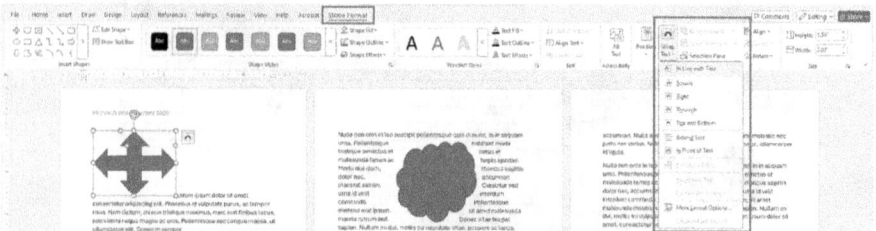

Figure 46.   *Wrap Text.png*

Anchoring Objects

1. Select the object and go to the **Layout Options** icon that appears next to it.

2. Choose a specific position on the page or relative to text.

3. Enable **Fix position on page** to keep the object in place, regardless of text changes.

3. GROUPING AND LAYERING OBJECTS

Grouping Objects

1. Select multiple objects by holding **Ctrl** (Windows) or **Command** (Mac) while clicking each object.

2. Right-click and choose **Group > Group** to combine them into one element.

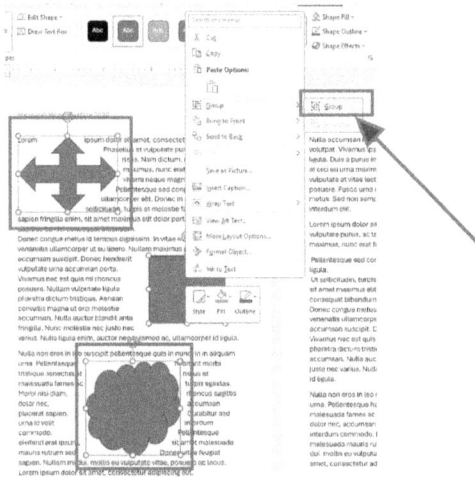

Layering Objects

1. Select an object and go to the **Shape Format** or **Picture Format** tab.

2. Use **Bring Forward** or **Send Backward** in the **Arrange** group to adjust the stacking order.

III. USING CHARTS

Charts visually represent data, making it easier to understand trends and comparisons.

Inserting a Chart

1. Go to the **Insert** tab and click **Chart** in the **Illustrations** group.

2. Choose a chart type, such as:

   » **Column**: Compare values across categories.

   » **Line**: Show trends over time.

   » **Pie**: Display proportions within a dataset.

Figure 47.   *Insert Chart.png*

3. Click **OK** to insert the chart and open an embedded Excel worksheet.

Editing Chart Data

1. Modify the data in the Excel worksheet.

2. Close the Excel window to update the chart in Word.

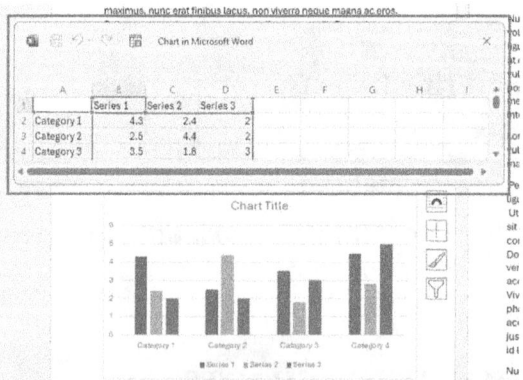

Customizing Chart Appearance

1. Select the chart to open the **Chart Tools** tab.

Figure 48.   *Edit Chart Data.png*

2. Use the **Design** and **Format** tabs to:
   - » Change chart styles and colors.
   - » Add or remove chart elements (e.g., axis titles, legends, data labels).
   - » Adjust the layout and positioning.

IV. PREPARING DOCUMENTS FOR PUBLISHING

Creating publish-ready documents requires attention to detail and careful preparation. Microsoft Word provides tools to ensure your document is polished, properly formatted, and optimized for its intended purpose.

1. FINALIZING LAYOUT AND CONTENT

Before printing or publishing, ensure your document is free of errors and visually consistent.

Steps to Review Layout and Content

1. **Proofread Thoroughly**:
   - » Use the **Review > Spelling & Grammar** tool to catch typos and grammatical errors.
   - » Read through the document manually to ensure clarity and accuracy.

2. **Check Consistency**:
   - » Verify uniform use of fonts, colors, and styles throughout the document.
   - » Ensure headers, footers, and page numbers are properly formatted and consistent.

3. **Preview the Document**:
   - » Go to **File > Print** to open the Print Preview screen.
   - » Examine margins, alignment, and overall layout.

2. PREPARING FOR DIGITAL PUBLISHING

When publishing your document online or sharing it digitally, consider converting it to a PDF or another compatible format.

Saving as PDF

1. Go to **File > Save As**.
2. Choose the location and select **PDF** from the **Save as Type** dropdown.
3. Click **Options** to customize settings:
   - » Optimize for **Standard (publishing online and printing)** or **Minimum size (publishing online only)**.
   - » Include non-printing elements like comments or markup if needed.
4. Click **Save** to generate the PDF.

Embedding Fonts for Portability

1. Go to **File > Options > Save**.
2. Check Embed fonts in the file under the Preserve fidelity when sharing this document section. This ensures your document appears the same on all devices, even if the fonts are not installed.

3. TIPS FOR PROFESSIONAL DOCUMENTS

- **Use High-Resolution Images**: Low-quality images may appear pixelated in print or online.
- **Keep File Sizes Manageable**: Optimize images and content to prevent excessively large file sizes.
- **Check Copyrights**: Ensure all content, especially images, complies with copyright laws.

CHAPTER 6: AUTOMATING & ADVANCED FEATURES

I. USING MAIL MERGE FOR LETTERS, LABELS, AND ENVELOPES

Mail Merge is a powerful feature in Microsoft Word that allows you to personalize letters, labels, and envelopes for multiple recipients efficiently. By combining a main document with a data source, you can automate the creation of customized documents.

1. WHAT IS MAIL MERGE?

Mail Merge connects your Word document to a data source (e.g., Excel spreadsheet, Access database) to populate fields like names, addresses, and other details.

Examples of Use Cases

- Personalizing invitation letters for a large group.
- Printing address labels for mailing campaigns.
- Creating envelopes with recipient information.

2. STEPS TO PERFORM MAIL MERGE

1. **Choose the Document Type**

    - Go to the **Mailings** tab.
    - Click **Start Mail Merge** and select the type of document:
        » **Letters**: For personalized letters.
        » **Email Messages**: For sending emails (requires Outlook).

>> **Envelopes** or **Labels**: For postal mailings.

>> **Directory**: For creating lists or catalogs.

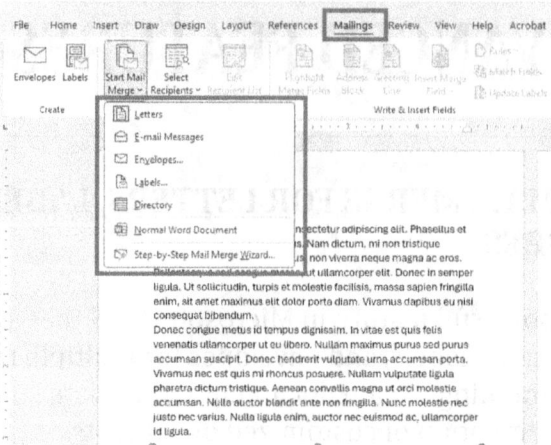

Figure 49.   Mail Merge Document Type.png

2. **Select a Data Source**

- Click **Select Recipients** in the **Mailings** tab.

- Choose an option:

  >> **Type a New List**: Enter recipient details directly into Word. After entering, you have to save the recipient details as a data source in order to continue.

  >> **Use an Existing List**: Browse and select an external data source (e.g., Excel file).

  >> **Choose from Outlook Contacts**: Use your Outlook contact list.

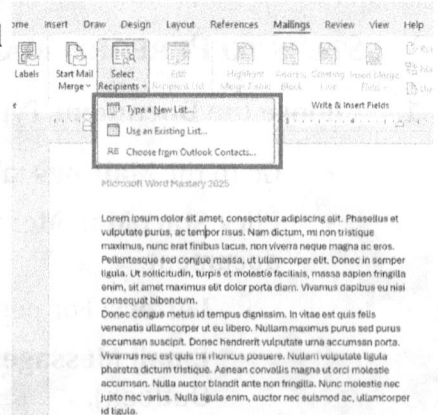

- Verify the data by clicking **Edit Recipient List** to ensure accuracy.

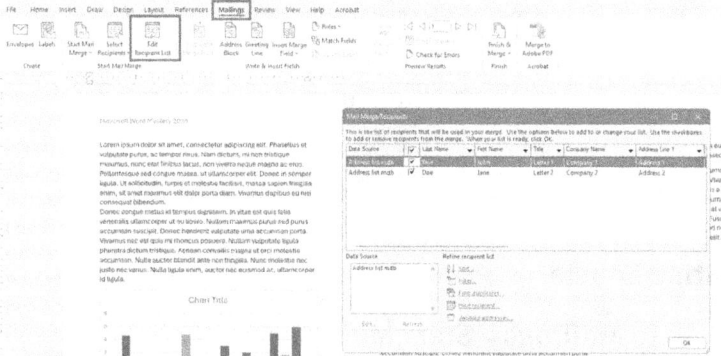

Figure 50.   *Edit Recipients.png*

3. Insert Merge Fields

- Place your cursor where you want personalized information to appear.
- Click **Insert Merge Field** in the **Mailings** tab.
- Select fields like **First Name**, **Last Name**, or **Address** to insert placeholders in the document.

4. Preview and Finalize

- Click **Preview Results** in the **Mailings** tab to view how the data populates the document.
- Use the navigation arrows to preview each recipient's document.

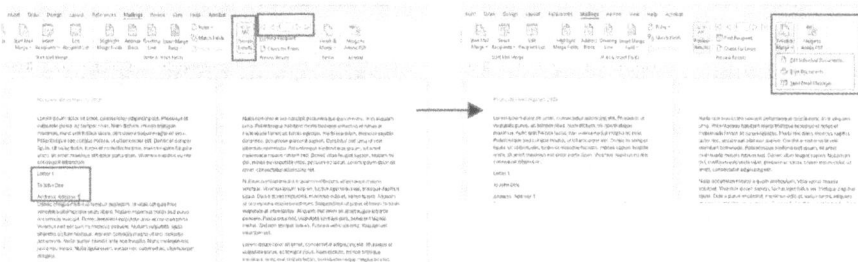

Figure 51.   *Mail Merge Preview and Finalize.png*

- Click **Finish & Merge** and choose:
  - » **Edit Individual Documents**: Create a separate

document for each recipient.

   » **Print Documents**: Send the merged documents directly to the printer.

   » **Send Email Messages**: Email the documents (if using the email option).

3. MAIL MERGE FOR LABELS AND ENVELOPES

Creating Labels

1. Go to **Mailings > Start Mail Merge > Labels**.
2. Select the label type and size from the dialog box.
3. Follow the same steps to select recipients and insert merge fields.
4. Preview the labels and print them using **Finish & Merge**.

Creating Envelopes

1. Go to **Mailings > Envelopes**.
2. Enter the return and recipient addresses or use merge fields for recipient details.
3. Click **Add to Document** to include the envelope in your main document.

4. TIPS FOR SUCCESSFUL MAIL MERGE

- **Organize Your Data Source**: Ensure the data source is clean and well-structured, with clear headers and no blank rows.
- **Test with a Few Records**: Preview a small batch of records to confirm the merge works.
- **Save Time with Templates**: Create reusable templates for letters, labels, and envelopes.

II. CREATING AND MANAGING MACROS TO AUTOMATE TASKS

Macros are powerful tools in Microsoft Word that automate repetitive tasks by recording a series of actions. By creating and managing macros, you can save time and increase efficiency in your workflow.

1. WHAT IS A MACRO?

A macro is a recorded sequence of commands and actions that can be played back to perform tasks automatically. Macros are especially useful for:

- Formatting documents consistently.

- Applying complex styles to text.

- Automating repetitive actions like inserting boilerplate text.

2. CREATING A MACRO

1. Go to the **View** tab and click **Macros** > **Record Macro**.

2. In the **Record Macro** dialog box:

   - Enter a name for the macro (e.g., "ApplyHeaderStyle").

Figure 52.   Set Macros Name.png

   - Choose where to store the macro:

     » **All Documents** (Normal.dotm): Makes the macro available in all Word documents.

     » **This Document**: Limits the macro to the current document.

- Assign a shortcut key or a button if desired.

3. Click **OK** to start recording.

4. Perform the actions you want the macro to automate. For example:

   - Format a heading.

   - Insert a specific table or logo.

   - Apply a particular style.

5. Once finished, go back to the **View** tab and click **Macros > Stop Recording**.

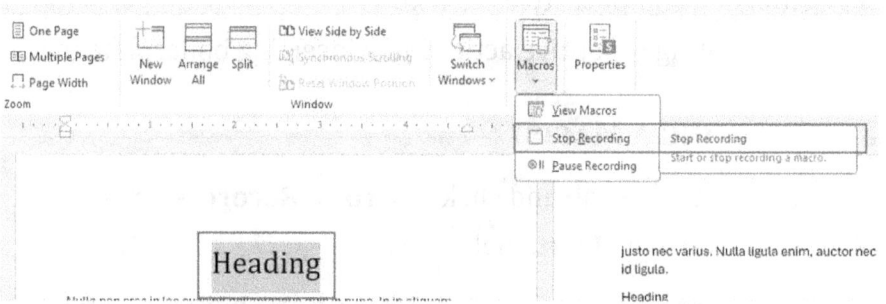

Figure 53.　　*Stop recording Macros.png*

3. RUNNING A MACRO

Using the Ribbon or Shortcut Key

1. Select the text where you want to apply the Macro.

2. Go to the **View** tab and click **Macros > View Macros**.

3. Select the macro you want to run and click **Run**.

4. If you assigned a shortcut key or button, use it to execute the macro directly.

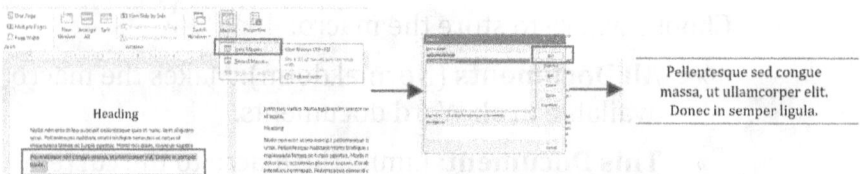

Figure 54.　　*Run a Macros.png*

4. MANAGING MACROS

Editing a Macro

Macros are written in VBA (Visual Basic for Applications). To edit a macro:

1. Go to the **View** tab and click **Macros > View Macros**.
2. Select the macro and click **Edit**.
3. Modify the VBA code in the editor. (Basic programming knowledge is helpful here.)

Deleting a Macro

1. Go to **View > Macros > View Macros**.
2. Select the macro you want to delete and click **Delete**.

5. SECURITY AND PERMISSIONS

Macros can contain harmful code, so it's important to manage security settings:

1. Go to **File > Options > Trust Center > Trust Center Settings**.
2. Select **Macro Settings** and choose the appropriate level:
   - » **Disable all macros without notification**: Safest option but prevents macros from running.
   - » **Disable all macros with notification**: Allows you to enable trusted macros.
   - » **Enable all macros**: Not recommended due to security risks.

III.   EMBEDDING AND LINKING OBJECTS

Embedding and linking objects in Microsoft Word allows you to integrate external content such as Excel charts or PowerPoint slides directly into your documents. These features are essential for creating dynamic and informative documents.

1. EMBEDDING OBJECTS

When you embed an object, it becomes part of the Word document, and you can edit it using its native application without needing the original file.

Steps to Embed an Object

1. Go to the **Insert** tab and click **Object** in the **Text** group.
2. In the **Object** dialog box, select the **Create from File** tab.
3. Click **Browse** to locate the file you want to embed (e.g., an Excel or PowerPoint file).
4. Check **Display as Icon** if you want to show an icon instead of the content.
5. Click **OK** to embed the object into your document.

Figure 55.   *Embed object.png*

Editing an Embedded Object

1. Double-click the embedded object to open it in its native application (e.g., Excel or PowerPoint).
2. Make changes and save them; the updates will appear in the Word document.

2. LINKING OBJECTS

Linking objects keeps the Word document connected to the original file. Updates to the source file are automatically reflected in the Word document.

Steps to Link an Object

1. Go to the **Insert** tab and click **Object** in the **Text** group.

2. In the **Object** dialog box, select the **Create from File** tab.

3. Click **Browse** to locate the file you want to link.

4. Check **Link to File** and click **OK**.

5. The linked content will appear in your document.

Editing a Linked Object

1. Right-click the linked object and choose **Linked Worksheet Object > Edit Link** (or a similar option depending on the object type).

2. Open the source file, make edits, and save it.

3. DIFFERENCES BETWEEN EMBEDDING AND LINKING

Feature	Embedding	Linking
Connection	Independent of the source file.	Dependent on the source file.
File Size	Larger, as the object is stored.	Smaller, as only a link is stored.
Updates	Static; doesn't reflect source changes.	Dynamic; reflects source changes.

IV. USING COPILOT IN WORD

Copilot is one of the major new additions to Microsoft Word. It serves as an intelligent writing assistant built directly into the app, helping you draft, summarize, rewrite, and transform content with simple prompts. Whether you are creating a document from scratch or refining an existing one, Copilot can significantly speed up your writing process.

Copilot works through the sidebar, the Home tab, or the sparkle icon that appears when you select text.

1. WHAT COPILOT CAN DO

Copilot supports a wide range of tasks, including:

- Summarizing long documents
- Rewriting existing text
- Transforming content into different formats
- Generating new text from a prompt
- Creating structured documents such as letters, proposals, and reports
- Drafting content based on uploaded files

These features help you produce high-quality writing with less effort and greater consistency.

2. SUMMARIZING CONTENT

Copilot can summarize either the entire document or only the text you select.

Steps to Summarize:

1. Go to the Home tab and click Copilot, or click the sparkle icon next to selected text.
2. Choose Summarize.
3. Select whether you want a brief, detailed, or bullet-point summary.

Summaries help you quickly understand key points and create concise overviews.

3. REWRITING TEXT

Rewrite suggestions improve clarity, tone, or structure without changing the meaning of your content.

How to Rewrite:

1. Highlight the text.
2. Click the sparkle icon or open Copilot.
3. Choose Rewrite and select one of the suggested versions.

You can insert the improved version directly or compare multiple alternatives before choosing.

4. TRANSFORMING CONTENT

Copilot can convert your content from one format to another.

- Convert bullet points into a paragraph
- Convert a paragraph into bullet points
- Turn rough notes into an email
- Turn a section into an executive summary
- Convert a block of text into a structured outline

Steps:

1. Select the text you want to transform.
2. Open Copilot → Transform.
3. Choose the format you want.

This is especially useful for repurposing content for different audiences.

5. GENERATING NEW TEXT

Copilot can draft new content using your instructions.

1. Open the Copilot sidebar.
2. Type a prompt such as: "Create a short introduction explaining the purpose of this report."

Copilot will generate a draft, which you can insert into your document and edit as needed.

6. Creating Structured Documents

Copilot can help you generate complete document structures. This is helpful when you know what you want to create but don't want to build the layout manually.

Example Prompt: "Create a one-page project proposal layout with sections for overview, objectives, timeline, and next steps."

Copilot will insert the structure and allow you to fill it in or ask for additional content.

7. Drafting From a File

You can instruct Copilot to create content from an existing document such as a Word file, PDF, or PowerPoint.

What Copilot Can Do with a File:

- Summarize the document
- Extract key points
- Rewrite the content in a different format
- Generate a new draft based on multiple files
- Create an outline of the document

Steps:

1. Open Copilot.
2. Write a prompt such as: "Summarize this PDF and rewrite it in a formal tone."

3. Attach or reference the file stored in OneDrive.

This feature is helpful when working with long reference materials or combining information from several sources.

8. DRAFTING FROM A PROMPT

If you don't have an existing document, Copilot can create content entirely from your instructions.

Examples of Prompts:

- "Draft an introduction for a classroom handbook."
- "Write a summary explaining the main updates in this policy."
- "Create a short paragraph describing our team's objectives."
- Copilot will generate text directly in the Word document.

9. LIMITATIONS, PRIVACY, AND DATA BEHAVIOR

While Copilot is powerful, it operates within Microsoft 365's security framework and has several built-in restrictions.

Limitations:

- Copilot cannot access files you do not have permission to open.
- It cannot bypass password-protected or restricted content.
- Offline mode disables Copilot completely.
- Complex formatting (tables, multi-column layouts, forms) may reduce accuracy.
- Very large files may result in partial or incomplete responses.

Privacy and Security:

- Copilot follows your organization's security and compliance policies.
- Content used with Copilot is not used to train public

Microsoft models.

- Copilot respects existing permissions and cannot see private information you cannot access.
- It cannot retrieve or expose hidden metadata unless visible in the document.

Good Practices:

- Always review Copilot output for accuracy.
- Confirm factual information, especially in legal, financial, and technical documents.
- Use Copilot to assist your writing, not replace your critical judgment.

CHAPTER 7: MANAGING & COLLABORATION

I.   COLLABORATING WITH MICROSOFT TEAMS

Microsoft Teams integrates with Word to enhance teamwork by centralizing communication and document sharing.

Steps to Collaborate Using Teams

1. Open Microsoft Teams and navigate to the desired team or channel.
2. Upload your Word document:
   » Click **Files** in the channel and select **Upload**.
3. Open the document in Teams by clicking on it.
4. Share the document link in the channel to notify team members.

Collaborating in Teams

- **Real-Time Editing**: Multiple users can edit the document simultaneously within Teams or Word Online.
- **Chat Integration**: Discuss changes with teammates using the chat feature alongside the document.
- **Commenting and Tracking**: Add comments and track changes directly within the document.

Integrating OneDrive and Teams

For optimal collaboration, combine OneDrive and Teams:

1. Save the document to OneDrive and upload it to Teams for shared access.

2. Changes made in Teams are automatically synced to OneDrive.

II.   REAL-TIME CO-AUTHORING AND TRACKING CHANGES

Real-time co-authoring and the ability to track changes are essential features in Microsoft Word for effective collaboration. They allow multiple users to work on the same document simultaneously while keeping a clear record of edits.

1.   REAL-TIME CO-AUTHORING

Real-time co-authoring enables multiple people to edit a document at the same time, with updates visible immediately.

Setting Up Real-Time Co-Authoring

1. Save your document to OneDrive or SharePoint: Go to **File > Save As** and choose OneDrive or SharePoint as the location.
2. Click **Share** in the top-right corner of Word.
3. Enter the email addresses of your collaborators and set permissions (**Can Edit** for editing access).
4. Click **Send** to share the document.

Editing Together in Real Time

- When collaborators open the document, their edits appear live.
- Each person's cursor is marked with their name, so you can see who is working on which section.

2.   TRACKING CHANGES

The **Track Changes** feature provides a clear view of all edits made to the document, allowing collaborators to accept or reject modifications.

Enabling Track Changes

1. Go to the **Review** tab and click **Track Changes** in the **Tracking** group.
2. Select **Simple Markup** to show changes in a clean, easy-to-read format or **All Markup** to display detailed edits.

Reviewing Changes

1. Navigate to the **Review** tab.
2. Use the **Next** and **Previous** buttons in the **Changes** group to move through edits.
3. Accept or reject each change by clicking **Accept** or **Reject**.

Customizing Track Changes

1. Go to **Review > Track Changes > Track Changes Options**.
2. Adjust settings for color coding, formatting, and which changes to track (e.g., insertions, deletions, or formatting changes).

III.   ADDING AND RESOLVING COMMENTS

Comments in Microsoft Word provide a simple and effective way for collaborators to give feedback, ask questions, or suggest changes. They are particularly useful in group projects.

Steps to Add a Comment

1. Highlight the text, object, or area where you want to add a comment.
2. Go to the **Review** tab and click **New Comment** in the **Comments** group.
3. Type your feedback or note in the comment box that appears in the margin.

Steps to Reply to a Comment

1. Click on the existing comment in the margin.

2. Click **Reply** inside the comment box and type your response.

3. Each reply will be nested under the original comment, keeping discussions organized.

Steps to Resolve a Comment

1. Click on the comment.

2. Select **Resolve** in the comment box. The comment will be marked as resolved but remains visible for reference.

Reopening a Resolved Comment

1. Click on the resolved comment.

2. Select **Reopen Thread** to continue the discussion.

Viewing All Comments

1. Go to the **Review** tab and click **Show Comments** in the **Comments** group.

2. The Comments Pane will appear, displaying all comments in the document.

Deleting Comments

1. To delete a single comment, right-click it and choose **Delete Comment**.

2. To delete all comments in the document: Go to **Review > Delete** and select **Delete All Comments in Document**.

IV.   PROTECTING YOUR FILES WITH WORD SECURITY FEATURES

Securing your documents is essential to protect sensitive information and maintain control over who can view, edit, or share your work. Microsoft Word provides robust security features to safeguard your files.

1. ADDING PASSWORD PROTECTION

Password-protecting your document ensures only authorized users can open or edit it.

Steps to Add a Password

1. Go to **File > Info > Protect Document**.
2. Select **Encrypt with Password**.
3. Enter a password in the dialog box and click **OK**.
4. Re-enter the password to confirm and click **OK** again. The document will now require the password to open.

Tips for Password Management

- Use a strong password combining letters, numbers, and symbols.
- Keep your password secure—Microsoft cannot recover it if forgotten.

2. RESTRICTING EDITING

Restricting editing limits what changes others can make to your document.

Steps to Restrict Editing

1. Go to **File > Info > Protect Document**.
2. Select **Restrict Editing**.
3. In the **Restrict Editing** pane:
   - » Check **Allow only this type of editing in the document**.
   - » Choose an option (e.g., No changes, Comments only, or Filling in forms).

4. Click **Yes, Start Enforcing Protection** and set a password to lock the restrictions.

3. MARKING A DOCUMENT AS FINAL

Marking a document as final notifies readers that the document is complete and discourages further editing.

Steps to Mark as Final

1. Go to **File > Info > Protect Document**.
2. Select **Mark as Final**.
3. Confirm the action when prompted. The document will become read-only, and a banner will appear indicating it is marked as final.

4. USING DIGITAL SIGNATURES

A digital signature verifies the authenticity of your document and confirms that it hasn't been tampered with.

Steps to Add a Digital Signature

1. Go to **File > Info > Protect Document**.
2. Select **Add a Digital Signature**.
3. Follow the prompts to set up or apply an existing digital signature.

5. INSPECTING AND REMOVING SENSITIVE INFORMATION

The **Document Inspector** helps identify and remove sensitive or hidden data before sharing.

Steps to Inspect a Document

1. Go to **File > Info > Check for Issues > Inspect Document**.
2. Select the types of data to inspect (e.g., Comments, Hidden

Text, or Document Properties).

3. Click **Inspect** and review the results.
4. Click **Remove All** to delete unwanted data.

V.   RECOVERING UNSAVED DOCUMENTS AND VERSION HISTORY

Losing unsaved work or needing to revert to an earlier version of a document can be frustrating. Microsoft Word offers tools to recover unsaved documents and access version history, ensuring you don't lose important content.

1.   RECOVERING UNSAVED DOCUMENTS

Word automatically saves temporary backups of your work, which can be recovered if the document wasn't saved before closing.

Steps to Recover Unsaved Documents

1. Open Word and go to **File > Info.**
2. Select **Manage Document > Recover Unsaved Documents.**
3. Browse the list of unsaved files in the dialog box.
4. Select the file you want to recover and click **Open.**
5. Save the recovered file immediately to avoid losing it again.

2.   USING AUTORECOVER

AutoRecover periodically saves your work in the background.

Enabling AutoRecover

1. Go to **File > Options > Save.**
2. Ensure **Save AutoRecover information every [X] minutes** is checked.
3. Set the desired time interval for AutoRecover saves.

If Word crashes or closes unexpectedly, the next time you open Word, it will display a list of recovered files in the **Document Recovery Pane**.

3. ACCESSING VERSION HISTORY

Word tracks changes to documents saved on OneDrive or SharePoint, allowing you to revert to earlier versions when needed.

Viewing and Restoring Previous Versions

1. Open the document saved in OneDrive or SharePoint.

2. Go to **File > Info**.

3. Click **Version History**.

4. A list of previous versions appears, including timestamps and editor names.

5. Select a version to open it.

6. To restore a version, click **Restore** or copy specific content into the current version.

4. TIPS FOR PREVENTING DATA LOSS

- **Save Regularly**: Use **Ctrl+S** (Windows) or **Command+S** (Mac) frequently to manually save your work.

- **Use OneDrive**: Save documents to OneDrive to take advantage of cloud-based autosaving and version history.

- **Set Shorter AutoRecover Intervals**: Adjust the AutoRecover frequency to 1-2 minutes for critical work.

CHAPTER 8:

WORD TOP SHORTCUTS

I.   ESSENTIAL SHORTCUTS FOR FASTER EDITING AND NAVIGATION

Keyboard shortcuts are powerful tools that can significantly speed up your workflow in Microsoft Word. By memorizing and using key combinations, you can save time and reduce reliance on the mouse.

CATEGORY	SHORTCUTS	FUNCTIONS
Basic Text Editing	Ctrl + C	Copy selected text or objects.
	Ctrl + X	Cut selected text or objects
	Ctrl + V	Paste copied or cut text or objects.
	Ctrl + Z	Undo the last action.
	Ctrl + Y	Redo the last undone action.
Formatting Text	Ctrl + B	Apply or remove bold formatting.
	Ctrl + I	Apply or remove italic formatting.
	Ctrl + U	Apply or remove underline formatting.
	Ctrl + Shift + >	Increase font size.
	Ctrl + Shift + <	Decrease font size.

CATEGORY	SHORTCUTS	FUNCTIONS
Navigation Shortcuts	Ctrl + Right Arrow / Left Arrow	Move the cursor by one word.
	Ctrl + Up Arrow / Down Arrow	Move the cursor by paragraphs.
	Home	Move the cursor to the beginning of the current line.
	End	Move the cursor to the end of the current line.
	Shift + Arrow Keys	Extend the selection by one character or line.
	Ctrl + Shift + Arrow Keys	Select by words or paragraphs.
	Ctrl + A	Select the entire document.
Managing Documents	Ctrl + N	Create a new document.
	Ctrl + O	Open an existing document.
	Ctrl + S	Save the current document.
	Ctrl + P	Open the print dialog.
	Ctrl + F	Open the Find tool.
	Ctrl + H	Open the Find and Replace tool.

II. CUSTOMIZING SHORTCUTS FOR YOUR WORKFLOW

Customizing keyboard shortcuts in Microsoft Word allows you to tailor your workflow to your specific needs. By assigning or modifying shortcuts, you can save time and streamline repetitive tasks.

Steps to Customize Shortcuts

1.   Go to **File > Options > Customize Ribbon**.

2. At the bottom of the window, click **Customize...** next to **Keyboard Shortcuts**.

3. The **Customize Keyboard** dialog box will appear, displaying categories and commands.

Steps to Assign a Shortcut

1. Select a category (e.g., **Home Tab**, **File Tab**) to find the command you want to customize.

2. Click on the command from the list.

3. In the **Press new shortcut key** box, press the key combination you want to assign. Example: Press **Ctrl + Alt + B** for creating border for all sides around the texts.

4. Click **Assign** to save the new shortcut.

5. Click **Close** to exit the customization menu.

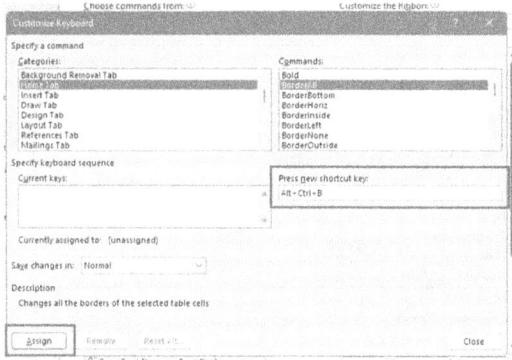

Figure 56.   *Assign New Shortcut.png*

Steps to Modify a Shortcut

1. Follow the same steps to access the **Customize Keyboard** dialog box.

2. Select the command with the existing shortcut.

3. In the **Current keys** box, click the shortcut you want to change.

4. Press a new key combination in the **Press new shortcut key** box.

5. Click **Assign** to update the shortcut.

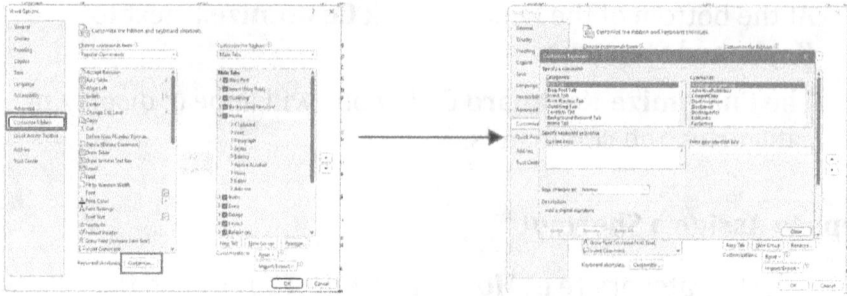

Figure 57.   *Customize Shortcuts.png*

Steps to Remove a Shortcut

1. Highlight the shortcut in the **Current keys** box.

2. Click **Remove** to delete the shortcut.

Saving Shortcuts to a Template

1. Customized shortcuts are saved in the current template (e.g., **Normal**).

2. To save shortcuts to a specific template: Select the template from the **Save changes in** dropdown in the **Customize Keyboard** dialog box.

Restoring Default Shortcuts

If you need to revert to Word's original shortcuts:

1. Open the **Customize Keyboard** dialog box.

2. Select **Reset All** to restore default shortcut settings.

3. Confirm the action to apply the changes.

CHAPTER 9:

TROUBLESHOOTING AND FAQS

I.   COMMON FORMATTING AND LAYOUT ISSUES

Formatting and layout problems are among the most common challenges users face in Microsoft Word. Understanding how to diagnose and resolve these issues can save time and frustration.

1.   TEXT DOESN'T ALIGN PROPERLY

Issue: Text alignment appears off, even after applying alignment settings.

Solution:
- Check paragraph settings:
    - » Highlight the text and go to the Home tab.
    - » Open the Paragraph dialog box (small arrow in the Paragraph group).
    - » Ensure alignment is set correctly (e.g., Left, Center, Right, or Justify).
- Check for unnecessary indents:
    - » In the **Paragraph** dialog box, ensure **Indentation** settings (Left and Right) are at zero unless needed.

2.   UNWANTED LINE BREAKS OR SPACING

Issue: Extra spacing appears between lines or paragraphs.

Solution:

- Adjust line spacing:
  - » Highlight the affected text.
  - » Go to **Home > Line and Paragraph Spacing** (in the **Paragraph** group).
  - » Select the desired spacing option (e.g., Single, 1.5, or Double).
- Remove extra paragraph spacing:
  - » Go to **Home > Line and Paragraph Spacing > Remove Space Before/After Paragraph**.
- Check for manual line breaks:
  - » Turn on **Show/Hide (¶)** in the **Home** tab.
  - » Look for manual line breaks and delete or replace them if necessary.

3. MARGINS APPEAR INCORRECT

Issue: Margins don't align as expected, affecting layout.

Solution:

1. Go to the **Layout** tab and click **Margins** in the **Page Setup** group.
2. Select a predefined margin or choose **Custom Margins**.
3. Ensure the settings match your document's requirements.

4. IMAGES OR OBJECTS DON'T STAY IN PLACE

Issue: Images or shapes move unexpectedly when editing.

Solution:

- Fix object position:
  - » Select the image or object.
  - » Go to the **Picture Format** or **Shape Format** tab and

click **Wrap Text**.

» Choose **Fix Position on Page** or adjust the wrapping style (e.g., Square, Tight, Behind Text).

- Anchor objects:
    » Right-click the object and choose **More Layout Options**.
    » Under the **Position** tab, set an anchor point.

5. TABLE LAYOUT ISSUES

Issue: Tables appear misaligned, or rows/columns don't resize as intended.

Solution:

- Align the table:
    » Select the table and go to the **Layout** tab (under **Table Tools**).
    » Use the alignment options in the **Table** group.
- Adjust row/column sizes:
    » Hover over the edge of a row or column until the resize cursor appears.
    » Drag to adjust, or go to **Table Tools > Layout > Cell Size** for precise dimensions.

6. TIPS FOR AVOIDING FORMATTING ISSUES

- **Use Styles**: Apply and modify styles to maintain consistent formatting throughout the document.
- **Check for Hidden Characters**: Enable **Show/Hide (¶)** to identify problematic spaces, tabs, or breaks.
- **Preview Before Printing**: Use **File > Print** to ensure layout accuracy.

II. RESOLVING COMPATIBILITY PROBLEMS

Compatibility issues can arise when working with older versions of Word, different file formats, or across platforms. Microsoft Word offers tools to identify and resolve these problems, ensuring smooth collaboration and document sharing.

1. FILE FORMAT INCOMPATIBILITY

Issue: A document created in a newer version of Word may not open or display correctly in an older version.

Solution:

- Save in a compatible format:
  - » Go to **File > Save As**.
  - » Choose **Word 97-2003 Document (*.doc)** from the **Save as Type** dropdown.
  - » Save the document for use in older versions of Word.
- Use the Compatibility Checker:
  - » Go to **File > Info > Check for Issues > Check Compatibility**.
  - » Review the list of potential issues and make adjustments as needed.

2. MISSING FONTS OR FORMATTING

Issue: Documents may appear different on another device due to unavailable fonts or formatting discrepancies.

Solution:

- Embed fonts.
- Use standard fonts: Stick to widely supported fonts like Arial, Times New Roman, or Calibri for better cross-platform compatibility.

3. MACROS AND ADD-INS NOT WORKING

Issue: Some macros or add-ins may not function across different Word versions or platforms.

Solution:

- Enable macros:
    - » Go to **File > Options > Trust Center > Trust Center Settings**.
    - » Select **Macro Settings** and enable the appropriate option (e.g., **Enable all macros**).
- Check compatibility of add-ins:
    - » Ensure the add-ins are updated to support the Word version in use.

4. UNSUPPORTED FEATURES IN WORD ONLINE

Issue: Some advanced features, such as macros or certain formatting options, are not available in Word Online.

Solution: Use the desktop app.
- » Open the document in Word Online.
- » Click **Open in Desktop App** to access the full range of features.

CONCLUSION

You've now journeyed through the ins and outs of Microsoft Word, equipping yourself with the skills to create, format, edit, and optimize your documents like a pro. Whether you're drafting reports, designing flyers, collaborating with a team, or automating tasks with macros, you have the knowledge to make Word work for you.

Key Takeaways:

- You've learned how to navigate Word's interface efficiently, making the most of tools like ribbons, toolbars, and shortcuts.

- Formatting and styling text is now a breeze, ensuring your documents look polished and professional.

- Advanced features like mail merge, collaboration tools, and templates have given you a competitive edge in document creation.

- With time-saving tips, automation techniques, and best practices, you can streamline your workflow and boost productivity.

But remember, mastering Microsoft Word is an ongoing process! With every update, new features emerge, making it even more powerful. Keep experimenting, stay curious, and don't hesitate to explore Word's online resources and communities to stay ahead.

Now it's time to put your skills to use—whether for work, school, or personal projects. Happy writing!

ABOUT THE AUTHOR

Ethan Wells is a seasoned finance and accounting professional with over 14 years of experience in auditing, corporate finance, financial management, and strategic consulting. After building a strong foundation in global corporations, Ethan transitioned into a pivotal consulting role, helping startups and innovative ventures achieve sustainable growth and financial success.

Driven by a passion for simplifying complex financial topics, Ethan writes practical, easy-to-understand guides designed for entrepreneurs, business owners, and professionals. His approachable style, combined with deep industry expertise, empowers readers to confidently navigate the evolving landscape of business, finance, and accounting.

Explore more titles in the Business Productivity Blueprint series to continue building your skills and boosting your productivity. From mastering Excel and Word to managing your business with QuickBooks and Office 365, there's a guide for every step of your journey.

www.ingramcontent.com/pod-product-compliance
Lightning Source LLC
Chambersburg PA
CBHW060934220326
41597CB00020BA/3825